The Peep of Day

F. L. Mortimer

FREE PRESBYTERIAN PUBLICATIONS

FREE PRESBYTERIAN PUBLICATIONS
133 Woodlands Road
Glasgow
G3 6LE

First Free Presbyterian Publications edition 1971

Second edition, revised and reset 1997

ISBN 0 902506 39 0

Printed by
Pioneer Press Limited
Skipton
North Yorkshire
BD23 2TZ

THE PEEP OF DAY

Preface

FROM very early on in her child's life, a godly mother will try to teach her child about our Creator and the Lord Jesus Christ, who came to be the Redeemer. And in due time she will make that instruction more systematic. This little work aims to convey systematic instruction to the child as soon as the child's mind is capable of receiving it. It may be at three years of age — it may not be till five — that the child is prepared to listen to these little lessons. But, sooner or later, he will give evidence of his immortality by willingly listening to teaching concerning the invisible, the eternal, the infinite.

The simplicity of the language may seem unworthy of the sublimity of the subject discussed in these pages and some may smile at the contrast, but the little one will not smile, for little children are capable of tasting higher pleasures than toys can afford. Happy is the community where the parents lead their little ones to the house of God, and lead them home again to read with them their little books and, verse by verse, the Book of Books!

It will be found that children can understand religious truths at a very early age; although the exact period is of course very different in different individuals. The child easily perceives that there must be a God, and acknowledges His power to be great; the only objections he raises to any doctrine are such, in general, as have never been solved by man, while the child finds no difficulty in believing that God's understanding is infinitely superior to his own.

And will it be deemed undesirable to instruct the child in religion when it is remembered that impressions made on the mind in early life are the most vivid and the most durable, that the readiest access is obtained to the young and tender heart, that wrong notions will be conceived by the ever-busy intellect, if left uninstructed, and that, life being uncertain, the eternal happiness of a child already knowing good from evil may be endangered by delay?

As it is clear that the greatest accuracy is essential in the foundation of a building, the writer has attempted to prove every statement either by the footnotes or by the references at the beginning of each chapter, both of which are intended solely for the use of the teacher. The poetry is also not designed to be learned by heart.

A verse applicable to each Scripture Lesson has been selected so that the child may memorise it after each lesson. Very young children will not be able to learn these verses till the second time of going through the lessons. Children should not be required to name the part of Scripture from which the words are taken.

•

Publisher's Note

In preparing this edition for the press, the publishers have taken the opportunity of revising it for two main reasons. Firstly in the interests of more careful expression at a number of points, and secondly to make its language rather simpler and more suitable for a time over a hundred years after it was first published. The above preface is an abridgement of the somewhat lengthy introductory material which the author supplied for the early editions of the book.

Contents

LESSON 1

The Body

CHILDREN, you have seen the sun in the sky. Who put the sun in the sky?

God.

Can you reach up so high?

No.

Who holds up the sun so that it does not fall?[1]

It is God.

God lives in heaven; heaven is much higher than the sun.[2]

Can you see God?

No.

Yet He can see you, for God sees everything.[3]

God made every thing at first, and God takes care of everything.[4]

God made you, my little child, and God takes care of you always.[5]

You have a little body. From your head down to your feet is what I call your body.

---

[1] 'Upholding all things by the word of His power.' Heb. 1:3.

[2] 'He ascended up far above all heavens.' Eph. 4:10.

[3] 'The eyes of the Lord are in every place, beholding the evil and the good.' Prov. 15:3.

[4] 'O Lord, Thou preservest man and beast.' Ps. 36:6.

[5] 'In Him we live, and move, and have our being.' Acts 17:28.

Put your hand in front of your mouth. What do you feel coming out of your mouth?

It is your breath. You breathe every moment. When you are asleep, you breathe. You cannot help breathing. But who gives you breath?[6]

God does every thing. God gave you this little body, and He makes it live, and move, and breathe.

There are bones in your body. God has made them strong and hard.[7] God made some bones for your arms and some bones for your legs. He made a bone for your back and more bones for your sides.

God has covered your bones with flesh. Your flesh is soft and warm. In your flesh there is blood. God has put skin outside,[8] and it covers your flesh and blood like a coat.

Now all these things, the bones and flesh and blood and skin are called your body. How kind it was of God to give you a body![9] I hope that your body will not get hurt.

Will your bones break?

Yes, they would, if you were to fall down from high up, or if a car were to go over them.

If you were to be very sick your flesh would waste away, and you would scarcely have anything left but skin and bones.

Did you ever see a child who had been sick a very long time?

I have seen a sick baby. It did not have round cheeks like yours, and a fat arm like this. The baby's flesh was almost gone, and its little bones were only covered with skin.

God has kept you strong and well.

How easy it would be to hurt your poor little body! If it were to fall into the fire, it would be burned up. If hot water were spilt on it, it would be scalded. If it were to fall into deep water, and it was not taken out very soon, it would be drowned. If a great knife were run through your body, the blood would come

---

[6] 'He that giveth breath unto the people upon it (the earth).' Isa. 42:5.

[7] 'Thou hast fenced me with bones.' Job 10:11.

[8] 'Thou hast clothed me with skin and flesh.' Job 10:11.

[9] 'I will praise Thee, for I am fearfully and wonderfully made.' Ps. 139:14.

out. If a great box were to fall on your head, your head would be crushed. If you were to fall out of the window, your neck would be broken. If you were not to eat some food for a few days, your little body would be very sick, your breath would stop, and you would grow cold, and you would soon be dead.

You see that you have a very weak little body.[10]

Can you keep your body from being sick, and from getting hurt?

You should try not to hurt yourself, but only God can keep your body from all harm — from fire and water, from wounds and bruises, and all kinds of sickness.[11] Kneel down and pray to God, 'Keep my poor little body from getting hurt.' God will hear you, and go on taking care of you.

My little body's made by God
Of soft warm flesh and crimson blood;
The slender bones are placed within,
And over all is laid the skin.

My little body's very weak;
A fall or blow my bones might break:
The water soon might stop my breath;
The fire might close my eyes in death.

But God can keep me by His care;
To Him I'll say this little prayer:
'O God, from harm my body keep,
Both when I wake and when I sleep.'

---

[10] '(They) that dwell in houses of clay . . . which are crushed before the moth.' Job 4:19.

[11] 'The Lord shall preserve thee from all evil.' Ps 121:7.

Questions

- Why does the sun not fall from the sky?
- What does God give you every moment?
- What are the four things that are called your body?
- How might your body be hurt?
- Who can keep it from being hurt?

Everything comes from God

A verse from the Bible for you to learn

God giveth to all life, and breath, and all things. Acts 17:25.

LESSON 2

A Mother's Care

I HAVE told you about your little body. Was your body always as big as it is now?

No. At one time it was very small indeed.

What were you called when your body was very small?

A baby.

Now you can take a little care of yourself, but then you could do nothing for yourself at all.

Can babies walk, or talk, or feed themselves, or dress themselves?

No.

But God gave you to someone who took great care of you when you were a baby. Who was it?

Your mother. She took care of you then. She nursed you in her arms and fed you. She took you out into the fresh air; she washed you and dressed you.

Do you love your mother?

Yes.

I know you do. But who gave you a mother?

It was God who gave you a kind mother.

A little while ago there was no such little creature as you.[1] Then God made your little body. And he gave you to your mother, who loved you as soon as she saw you. It was God who made your mother love you so much,[2] and made her so kind to you.

Your kind mother dressed your poor little body in neat clothes and laid you down in a cradle.

When you cried she gave you food and hushed you to sleep in her arms. She showed you pretty things to make you smile. She held you up and showed you how to move your feet. She taught you to speak, and she often kissed you and called you sweet names.

Is your mother still kind to you?

Yes, she is, though she is sometimes angry.

But she wishes to make you good; that is why she is sometimes a little angry. I know she will be kind to you as long as she lives.

But remember who gave you this mother. God sent you to a dear mother instead of putting you in the fields, where no one would have seen you or taken care of you.

Can your mother keep you alive?

No.

She can feed you, but she cannot make your breath go on.

God thinks of you every moment.[3] If He were to forget you, your breath would stop.

Do you ever thank your mother for her kindness?

---

[1] 'We are but of yesterday.' Job 8:9.

[2] 'God had brought Daniel into favour and tender love with the prince.' Dan. 1:9.

[3] 'Are not five sparrows sold for two farthings, and not one of them is forgotten before God ? But even the very hairs of your head are all numbered.' Luke 12:6, 7.

Yes. You often say, 'Thank you,' and sometimes you put your arms round her neck and say, 'I do love you so much, dear mother!' Will you not thank God who gave you a mother, and who keeps you alive? You should kneel down when you speak to God; then you should say, 'O God, how good Thou hast been to me! I want to thank Thee.'

Would God hear your little thanks?

Yes, God would hear, and be pleased.[4]

Who fed me from her gentle breast,
And hushed me in her arms to rest,
And on my cheeks sweet kisses pressed?
My Mother.

When sleep forsook my open eye,
Who was it sang sweet hush-a-by;
And rocked me that I should not cry?
My Mother.

Who sat and watched my infant head,
When sleeping on my cradle bed,
And tears of sweet affection shed?
My Mother.

When pain and sickness made me cry,
Who gazed upon my heavy eye,
And wept for fear that I should die?
My Mother.

Who ran to help me when I fell,
And would some pretty story tell,
Or kiss the place to make it well?
My Mother.

---

[4] 'I will praise the name of God with a song, and will magnify him with thanksgiving. This also shall please the Lord better than an ox, or bullock, that hath horns and hoofs.' Ps. 69:30, 31.

Who taught my infant lips to pray,
And love God's holy Book and day,
And walk in wisdom's pleasant way?
My Mother.

And can I ever cease to be
Affectionate and kind to her,
Who was so very kind to me?
My Mother.

Ah no, the thought I cannot bear,
And if God please my life to spare,
I hope I shall reward your care,
My Mother.

When you are feeble, old, and grey,
My healthy arm shall be your stay,
And I will soothe your pains away,
My Mother.

And when I see you hang your head,
'Twill be my turn to watch your bed,
And tears of sweet affection shed,
My Mother.

For God, who lives above the skies,
Would look with vengeance in His eyes,
If ever I should dare despise
My Mother.

Questions

- What was it your mother did for you when you were a baby?
- Does your mother make you breathe and keep you alive?
- Why did God give you a mother?
- What should you say to God for giving you a mother?

We should thank God

A verse from the Bible for you to learn

O give thanks unto the Lord; for He is good. Ps. 136:1.

LESSON 3

A Father's Care

WHO dresses you and feeds you?

Your dear mother.

But how does your mother get money to buy your clothes and your food?

Father brings it home.

How does your father get money?

He works all day long, and he gets money and brings it home to mother. He says to your mother, 'Buy some food with this money, and use some of it for the children.' Will your father give his money to buy food for you?

Yes, and it is very kind of him. Do you love your father?

Of course you do.

Why does your father go out to his work?

So that you may have plenty of food. While he is working, he often thinks of you, and he hopes that he will find you a good child when he comes home. You are glad to see him, I know. Sometimes you run to meet him, and when he sits down you climb on his knee.

Who made your father love you at first?

It was God.

Your father loves you very much, so he gives you all you need. He pays some of his money for a house so that you can live in it with him.

If your father were to die, what would you do, for you would then be a fatherless child?

Could your father die?

Oh yes, some little children have no father. I have heard of a little child whose father fell down from a high ladder and was killed. Another child's father was kicked by a horse and died. Some children's fathers fall sick and die.

Perhaps your father may die, but God can keep him alive. You can pray to God to keep him alive. In the morning you can say, 'O God, let Father come home safely this evening.'

But if God were to let your father die, you would still have one Father left. Who do I mean? What do you say to God in your prayer?

'Our Father, which art in heaven.'

Yes, if you are one of God's children you have a Father in heaven, besides the father you have at home, for God is your Father.*

Can your heavenly Father die?

No, never.

Does He love you?

Yes. He loves you even more than your other father does.[1] He is always thinking of you. He is always looking at you. He gives you many good things. He will take you to live with Him in heaven some day.[2]

Let us think of the things which God has given you. Let us count them:

---

* God is our Father in Creation; man has lost this great favour through sin, but it is restored in the gospel: Have we not all one father? hath not one God created us?' Mal. 2:10. 'Ye are of your father the devil, and the lusts of your father, ye will do.' John 8:44, and '. . . but ye have received the Spirit of adoption, whereby we cry, Abba, Father.' Rom. 8:15.

[1] 'When my father and my mother forsake me, then the Lord will take me up.' Ps. 27:10.

[2] 'God our Saviour, who will have all men to be saved, and to come unto the knowledge of the truth.' 1 Tim. 2:3, 4.

1. Father, to work for you.
2. Mother, to take care of you.
3. A house to live in.
4. A bed to sleep in.
5. Fire to warm you.
6. Clothes to wear.
7. Food to eat.
8. Breath every moment.

Questions

- What is it your father does to get money?
- Why does he buy things for you with his money?
- What sad things have happened to some children's fathers?
- Is there a Father that cannot die?

God is full of pity

A verse from the Bible for you to learn

Like as a father pitieth his children, so the Lord pitieth them that fear Him. Ps. 103:13.

LESSON 4

The Soul

HAS God been kind to dogs? Has He given them bodies?

Yes.

Have they bones and flesh and blood and skin?

Yes.

The dog has a body as well as you. Is the dog's body like yours?

No.

How many legs have you?

Two.

How many legs has the dog?

Four.

Have you got arms?

Yes, two.

Has the dog got arms?

No; it has no arms or hands. But the dog has legs instead.

Your skin is smooth, but the dog is covered with hair.

Is the cat's body like yours?

No; it is covered with fur.

Is a chicken's body like yours? How many legs has the chicken?

Two.

And so have you. But are its legs like yours?

No; the chicken has very thin legs, and has claws instead of feet.

Have you feathers on your skin? Have you wings? Is your mouth like a chicken's beak? Has the chicken any teeth?

No; the chicken's body is not at all like yours. Yet the chicken has a body, for it has flesh and bones and blood and skin.

Has a fly got a body?

Yes, it has a black body, and six black legs, and two wings like glass. Its body is not at all like yours.

Who gave bodies to dogs, horses, chickens and flies? Who keeps them alive?

God thinks of all these creatures every moment.[1]

Can a dog thank God?

No, dogs and horses, sheep and cows, cannot thank God.

Why can they not thank God? Is it because they cannot talk?

That is not the only reason.

The real reason is, they cannot think of God. They have never heard about God. They cannot understand about God.[2]

---

[1] 'Are not five sparrows sold for two farthings, and not one of them is forgotten before God?' Luke 12:6.

[2] 'Be ye not as the horse or the mule, which have no understanding.' Ps. 32:9.

Why not?

Because they have no souls like yours.

Have you got a soul?

Yes, in your body there is a soul which will never die. Your soul can think about God. When God made your body, He put your soul inside. Are you glad of that? When God made the dogs, He put no soul like yours inside their bodies, and they cannot think of God.

Can I see your soul?

No, I cannot see it. No one can see it but God.[3] He knows what you are thinking about just now.

Which is better, your soul or your body?

Your soul is much better.

Why is your soul better than your body?

Your body can die, but your soul cannot die.[4]

Shall I tell you what your body is made of?

Dust. God made the dust into flesh and blood.

How was your soul made?

Your soul is made of the breath of God.[5]

That little dog will die some day. Its body will be thrown away.[6] The dog will be quite gone when its body is dead. But when your body dies, your soul will be alive for ever.[7]

Where would you be put if you were dead?

Your body would be put in a hole in the ground, but your soul would not be in the hole.[8]

Even a baby has a soul, or a spirit.

---

[3] 'Thou, even Thou only, knowest the hearts of all the children of men.' 1 Kings 8:39.

[4] 'What shall a man give in exchange for his soul?' Matt. 16:26.

[5] 'And the Lord God formed man of the dust of the ground, and breathed into his nostrils the breath of life; and man became a living soul.' Gen. 2:7.

[6] 'The beasts that perish.' Ps. 49:20.

[7] 'Who knoweth the spirit of man that goeth upward, and the spirit of the beast that goeth downward to the earth?' Eccles. 3:21.

[8] 'Then shall the dust return to the earth as it was: and the spirit shall return unto God who gave it.' Eccles. 12:7.

One day as I was walking in the streets, I saw a man carrying a box. Some people were walking behind and crying. There was a dead baby in the box. Was the soul of the baby in the box?

No, its soul had gone up to God.'[9]

Will you not thank God for giving you a spirit? Will you not ask Him to take your spirit to live with Him when your body dies?[10] Say to God, 'Take my spirit to live with Thee when my body dies and turns into dust.'

What is that part which can't decay?

It is your soul.

Your body will decay; it will turn into dust. But your soul will live for ever; it will never decay.

Questions

- What other things have bodies, as well as you?
- Are their bodies like yours?
- What have you besides a body?
- Why cannot dogs and horses think of God?
- Is your soul better than your body?
- Why?
- What is your body made of?
- What is your soul made of?
- Where will your body be put when you die?
- Where do you hope that your soul will go?

What happens to us when we die?

A verse from the Bible for you to learn

Then shall the dust return to the earth as it was: and the spirit shall return unto God who gave it. Eccles. 12:7.

---

[9] 'I shall go to him, but he shall not return to me.' 2 Sam. 12:23.

[10] 'We are . . . willing rather to be absent from the body, and to be present with the Lord.' 2 Cor. 5:8.

LESSON 5

The Good Angels

YOU know that God lives in heaven. He has no body, for He is a spirit.[1] Does He live in heaven alone?

No; angels stand all around His throne.[2]

What are angels?

Angels are spirits.[3] They are bright like the sun,[4] but they are not so bright as God, for He is brighter than the sun.[5] The angels are always looking at God,[6] and it is God that makes them shine so brightly.

They sing sweet songs about God.[7] They say, 'How good God is! How wise! How great!' There is no night in heaven.[8] The angels are never tired of singing, and they never need to sleep.[9]

They are never sick, and they will never die. They never weep; there are no tears on their cheeks, but sweet smiles, for angels are always happy.[10]

---

[1] 'God is a Spirit.' John 4:24.

[2] 'All the angels stood round about the throne.' Rev. 7:11.

[3] 'Who maketh His angels spirits.' Ps. 104:4.

[4] 'His countenance was like lightning.' Matt. 28:3.

[5] 'I saw in the way a light from heaven, above the brightness of the sun.' Acts 26:13.

[6] 'Their angels do always behold the face of My Father which is in heaven.' Matt. 18:10.

[7] 'I heard the voice of many angels saying with a loud voice, Worthy is the Lamb . . . . And every creature which is in heaven . . . heard I saying, Blessing, and honour, and glory, and power, be unto Him that sitteth upon the throne and unto the Lamb for ever and ever.' Rev. 5:11, 12, 13.

[8] 'There shall be no night there.' Rev. 22:5.

[9] It is said of the four beasts (which certainly represent saints), 'That they rest not day and night, saying, Holy, holy, holy, Lord God Almighty.' Rev. 4:8. Angels 'excel in strength.' Ps. 103:20.

[10] It is said of the saints, 'God shall wipe away all tears from their eyes; and there shall be no more death, neither sorrow, nor crying, neither shall there be any more pain.' Rev. 21:4. And the saints will then be 'equal unto the angels.' Luke 20:35, 36.

If the angels were bad, they would be unhappy. To do wrong always makes people unhappy.

The angels are completely good.[11] They love God very much, and listen to all that He says.[12]

They have wings,[13] and can fly very quickly.[14] God sends them down here to take care of His children.[15] As soon as God tells an angel to go, he begins to fly.[16] They are very strong, and can keep us from harm.[17]

Do you want the angels to be near you at night? Do you know this nice verse?

> I lay my body down to sleep,
> Let angels guard my head,
> And through the hours of darkness keep
> Their watch around my bed.

You must ask God to send the angels, for they never go, except when God sends them.[18]

God is their Father.[19] He is their only Father. The angels are the children of God, and live in God's house in heaven. If you do what God tells you, you are like the angels who obey God.

---

[11] God 'spared not the angels that sinned, but cast them down to hell.' 2 Pet. 2:4.

[12] 'Bless ye the Lord, all ye His hosts, ye ministers of His, that do His pleasure.' Ps. 103:21.

[13] 'Above it stood the seraphims: each one had six wings.' Isa. 6:2.

[14] 'The man Gabriel . . . being caused to fly swiftly.' Dan. 9:21.

[15] 'Are they not all ministering sprits, sent forth to minister for them who shall be heirs of salvation?' Heb. 1:14.

[16] '(They) do His commandments, hearkening unto the voice of His word.' Ps. 103:20.

[17] '(Angels) shall bear thee up in their hands, lest thou dash thy foot against a stone.' Ps. 91:12.

[18] 'Thinkest thou that I cannot now pray to My Father, and He shall presently give me more than twelve legions of angels?' Matt. 26:53.

[19] 'Where wast thou when I laid the foundations of the earth? When the morning stars sang together, and all the sons of God shouted for joy?' Job 38:4, 7.

The angels wish us to grow good and to come to live with them in heaven.[20] When a child is sorry for its naughtiness, and prays to God to forgive it, the angels are very pleased.[21]

When a little child who loves God falls sick, and is going to die, God says to the angels, 'Go and bring that little child's soul up to heaven.'[22] Then the angels fly down, the little darling shuts its eyes, it lays its head on its mother's bosom, its breath stops, the child is dead. Where is its soul? The angels are carrying it up to heaven.

How happy the child is now! Its pain is over; it is grown completely good;[23] it is bright like an angel.[24] It holds a harp in its hand, and begins to sing a sweet song of praise to God.[25] Its little body is put into a grave, and turns into dust. But one day God will make its body alive again.

Dear children, will you pray to God to send His angels to fetch your souls when you die?

Around God's glorious throne above
The happy angels stand,
And ever praise the God they love,
And fly at His command.

Their faces, like the sun, are bright,
And sweetest smiles they wear;
They never sleep; there is no night,
Nor need of candle there.

---

[20] 'Take heed that ye despise not one of these little ones; for I say unto you, That in heaven their angels do always behold the face of My Father which is in heaven.' Matt. 18:10.

[21] 'There is joy in the presence of the angels of God over one sinner that repenteth. Luke 15:10.

[22] 'And it came to pass, that the beggar died, and was carried by the angels into Abraham's bosom.' Luke 16:22.

[23] 'The spirits of just men made perfect.' Heb. 12:23.

[24] 'Then shall the righteous shine forth as the sun in the kingdom of their Father.' Matt. 13:43.

[25] 'I heard the voice of harpers harping with their harps. These were redeemed from among men.' Rev. 14:2, 4.

Questions

- Who live with God in heaven?
- What are the angels always doing?
- Why are they always happy?
- Why do angels come down here?
- What do the angels do for children who love God, when they die?
- Can you make yourself good?

God tells His angels to take care of His children

A verse from the Bible for you to learn

He shall give His angels charge over thee, to keep thee in all thy ways. Ps. 91:11.

LESSON 6

The Wicked Angels

WHEN did God begin to live in heaven?

God always lived in heaven.[1]

Once there was no such little child as you, but there always was God. Once there was no sun, but there always was God. Once there were no angels,[2] but there always was God.

---

[1] 'From everlasting to everlasting Thou art God.' Ps. 90:2.

[2] 'By Him were all things created, that are in heaven, and that are in earth, visible and invisible.' Col. 1:16.

No one made God; God was before all things, and God made every thing. A very long time ago God made the angels. How many angels did he make?

No one can tell how many. There were more than could be counted.[3] They were all good and happy.

But some of the angels grew bad. They stopped loving God, and grew proud and disobedient.

Would God let them stay in heaven after they were bad?

No; He cast them out, and put them in chains and darkness.[4]

One of these bad angels was called Satan. He is the chief, or prince, of the bad angels. He is also called the Devil.[5] The Devil is very wicked,[6] and hates God. He can never go back to heaven again,[7] but he comes here where we live,[8] and he brings the other devils with him.[9]

We cannot see Satan, because he is a spirit, but he is always walking about, and trying to make people bad.[10] Satan loves doing harm to people; he does not wish to be good. It pleases Satan to see people in pain and in tears;[11] but it pleases him

---

[3] 'An innumerable company of angels.' Heb. 12:22.

[4] 'The angels which kept not their first estate, but left their own habitation, He hath reserved in everlasting chains under darkness unto the judgment of the great day.' Jude 6.

[5] 'The old serpent, called the Devil, and Satan, which deceiveth the whole world: he was cast out into the earth, and his angels were cast out with him.' Rev.12:9. 'The prince of the power of the air.' Eph. 2:2.

[6] 'The devil sinneth from the beginning.' 1 John 3:8.

[7] 'And the angels which kept not their first estate . . . he hath reserved in everlasting chains.' Jude 6.

[8] 'Then Satan answered the Lord, and said, From going to and fro in the earth, and from walking up and down in it.' Job 1:7

[9] Satan 'was cast out into the earth, and his angels were cast out with him.' Rev. 12:9.

[10] 'The spirit that now worketh in the children of disobedience.' Eph. 2:2.

[11] 'In mine adversity they rejoiced.' Ps. 35:15. 'Thou lovest evil more than good.' Ps. 52:3. 'He loved cursing.' Ps. 109:17. All that is said of the wicked applies in a higher degree to Satan as the author of sin, for Christ said to the wicked. 'Ye are of your father the devil, and the lusts of your father ye will do.' John 8:44.

best to see them wicked, because then he thinks that they will come and live with him in his dark place. He hopes there will be very many people in hell, so he tries to make us do wicked things and to keep us from praying to God.[12]

I cannot tell you how very bad Satan is. He is very cruel, for he likes to give pain.[13] He is a liar, and teaches people to tell lies.[14] He is proud,[15] and wishes people to think more of him than of God. He is jealous, and cannot bear to see people happy for ever.[16]

The devil hopes very much that you will come and live with him when you die. He knows that, if you are bad like him, you will live with him in hell. So he tries to make you like himself. When you are angry, you are like the devil. When you say, 'I don't care,' you are like the devil. When you think yourself good, you are proud like the devil.

Can God keep you from listening to the devil?

Yes, he can; for God is a great deal stronger than Satan.'[17] *Besides this, God is always near you, for God is everywhere. Now Satan cannot be everywhere at the same time. It is true that Satan has a great many angels who go where he tells them; and that Satan and his angels come near you very often. But God is always with you; He is in front of you and behind you and on every side of you; He is about your bed when you

---

[12] 'Simon, behold, Satan hath desired to have you, that he may sift you as wheat.' Luke 22:31. 'But if our gospel be hid, it is hid to them that are lost: in whom the god of this world hath blinded the minds of them which believe not.' 2 Cor. 4:3, 4.

[13] Satan is called 'a roaring lion.' 1 Pet. 5:8. His 'fiery darts' are spoken of in Eph. 6:16.

[14] 'He is a liar, and the father of it.' John 8:44.

[15] 'All these things will I give Thee, if Thou wilt fall down and worship me.' Matt. 4:9.

[16] This is proved by Satan having ruined man, and by his continuing to tempt him.

[17] 'O Lord God of hosts, who is a strong Lord like unto Thee?' Ps. 89:8.

* To Teachers. A very young child would not understand the rest of this chapter, except the last sentence. Therefore, it would be better to miss out this passage when the pupil is very young.

sleep, and about your path when you walk.[18] Therefore you do not need to be afraid of Satan; only ask God to help you, and He will do so.

Satan is much stronger than you are;[19] but God is stronger than everyone. If anybody were to come to hurt you when you were alone, you would be frightened; but if you saw your father coming, you would run to him and you would not be frightened any more. Now God is stronger than your father; He can keep Satan from hurting you. Pray to Him, and say, 'O Lord, keep me from being wicked like the devil, and from going to hell.'[20]

God lives on high beyond the sky,
And angels bright all clothed in white,
The praises sing of heaven's King.
This God can see both you and me;
Can see at night as in the light;
And all we do remembers too.
'Tis He bestows my food and clothes,
And my soft bed to rest my head,
And home so neat and mother sweet.
And should not I —or ever try
To do what He has ordered me,
And dearly love this Friend above?
I always should be very good:
At home should mind my parents kind;
At school obey what teachers say.
Now if I fight and scratch, and bite,
In passions fall and bad names call,
Full well I know where I shall go.
Satan is glad when I am bad,

---

[18] 'Thou compassest my path and my lying down, and art acquainted with all my ways. . . . Thou hast beset me behind and before.' Ps. 139:3, 5.

[19] 'For we wrestle not against flesh and blood, but against principalities, against powers.' Eph. 6:12.

[20] 'Resist the devil, and he will flee from you.' James 4:7.

And hopes that I with him shall lie
In fire and chains and dreadful pains.
All liars dwell with him in hell,
And many more who cursed and swore,
And all who did what God forbid.
And I have not done what I ought;
I am not fit with God to sit,
And angels bright all clothed in white.
I will confess my wickedness,
And will entreat for mercy sweet.
O Lord, forgive and let me live.
My body must be turned to dust.
Then let me fly beyond the sky,
And see Thy face in that sweet place.

Questions

- Did the angels always live in heaven?
- Who has lived always?
- Why did God cast some of the angels out of heaven'?
- What is the name of the prince of the bad angels?
- Why does Satan walk about here?
- Can you keep yourselves from Satan?

God punished the wicked angels

A verse from the Bible for you to learn

God spared not the angels that sinned, but cast them down to hell, and delivered them into chains of darkness. 2 Pet. 2:4.

LESSON 7

The World

PART 1 — GENESIS 1:1-10

THIS large place we live in is called the world. It is very beautiful. If we look up we see the blue sky; if we look down we see the green grass. The sky is like a curtain spread over our heads, the grass like a carpet under our feet, and the bright sun is like a very bright light. It was very kind of God to make such a beautiful world, and to let us live in it.

God was in heaven, and all His bright angels around Him, when He began to make the world.[1] God's Son was with Him, for God always had a Son,[2] just like Himself.[3]

His Son's name is Jesus Christ. He is as good and great as God His Father. The Father and the Son are God. They always lived together, and They love each other perfectly.[4] The Father and the Son are one God, and They made the world.[5] How did God make the world?

By speaking. First of all, God made the light. God said, 'Let there be light,' and there was light. No one but God can make things by speaking. God made things out of nothing. He only spoke, and the light came.[6]

---

[1] 'Where wast thou when I laid the foundations of the earth . . . and all the sons of God shouted for joy?' Job 38:4, 7.

[2] 'I was set up from everlasting, from the beginning, or ever the earth was. . . . When He appointed the foundations of the earth, then I was by Him.' Prov. 8:23, 29, 30.

[3] 'The express image of His person.' Heb. 1:3.

[4] 'I was daily His delight.' Prov. 8:30. 'But that the world may know that I love the Father.' John 14:31.

[5] 'In the beginning was the Word, and the Word was with God, and the Word was God. . . . All things were made by Him.' John 1:1, 3.

[6] 'Through faith we understand that the worlds were framed by the word of God, so that things which are seen were not made of things which do appear.' Heb. 11:3.

Then God made the air. You cannot see the air, but you can feel it. The air is everywhere. You can sometimes hear the noise it makes, for you hear the wind blow, and the wind is air.

Next God put some water up very high. The clouds are full of water; and sometimes the water comes down, and we call it rain.

God made a large, deep place and filled it with water. God spoke to the water, and it rushed into the deep place. God called this water the sea.[7]

The sea is very large, and it is always moving up and down, and tossing itself about. But it cannot get out of the large, deep place in which God has put it; for God said, 'Stay there.'[8] When the wind blows hard, the sea makes a loud noise, and roars.

God made some dry land for us to walk upon. We call it ground. We could not walk on the sea or build houses on the sea; but the ground is hard and firm and dry.

Now I have told you of five things that God made:

1. The light.
2. The air.
3. The clouds.
4. The sea.
5. The dry land.

Let us praise God for making such a large and beautiful world.

'Twas God who made this world so fair,
The shining sun, the sky, the air;
'Twas God who made the sea, the ground,
And all the things I see around.

---

[7] 'The waters stood above the mountains. At Thy rebuke they fled . . . they go down by the valleys, unto the place which Thou hast founded for them.' Ps. 104:6-8.

[8] 'And (I) brake up for it My decreed place, and set bars and doors, and said, Hitherto shalt thou come, but no further: and here shall thy proud waves be stayed.' Job 38:10, 11.

When He began the world to make,
These were the mighty words He spake;
'Let there be light.' His voice was heard:
And the obedient light appeared.

The angels saw the light arise,
And with their praises filled the skies.
'How great our God, how wise, how strong!'
Such is their never-ending song.

Questions

- What is this place that we live in called?
- Who was always in heaven with God?
- Is Jesus Christ the same as God?
- How did God make this world?
- What was the first thing that God made?
- What can you feel but cannot see?
- What is the water in the sky called?
- What is the name of the large deep place full of water?
- What do we walk on?
- What are the first five things that God made?

How light was made

A verse from the Bible for you to learn

And God said, Let there be light: and there was light.
Gen. 1:3.

LESSON 8

The World

PART 2 — GENESIS 1:11-19

WHEN God made the dry land, there was nothing on it. It was bare.

So God spoke, and things grew out of the ground. Trees came out of it; they were covered with green leaves of different shapes. Some were called oak trees, and some were called elm trees, and some were called beech trees. Some trees bore nice fruit, such as plum trees, apple trees, orange trees and fig trees.

Vegetables grew out of the earth. Potatoes and beans, cabbages and lettuces, are called vegetables.

Corn came out of the earth. Some corn is called wheat, and some corn is called barley, and some is called oats. The ears of corn bend down when they are ripe; then they look yellow like gold.

God made the soft green grass to spring up, and flowers to grow among the grass — flowers of all colours, and of the sweetest smell. The yellow buttercup, the white lily, the blue violet — and the rose, the most beautiful of all flowers.

I have told you of five sorts of things that grow out of the earth:

1. Trees.
2. Vegetables.
3. Corn.
4. Grass.
5. Flowers.

The world looked very beautiful when it was covered with grass and trees. But only God and the angels saw its beauty.

Afterwards God placed the sun in the sky. He made it shine all day long and go from one end of the world to the other.[1]

---

[1] God demands of Job, 'Hast thou commanded the morning since thy days; and caused the dayspring to know his place?' Job 38:12.

God made the moon to shine at night, and He covered the sky with stars.

You never saw anything as bright as the sun. It is very large indeed, only it looks small, because it is a very long way off. It cannot fall, for God holds it up.[2] God makes it move across the sky. The moon does not shine as brightly as the sun, for God lets it be dark at night, so that we may rest, and sleep soundly.[3]

Who can count the stars?

No one but God.[4] He knows their names and their number, too.[5] When we look at the moon and stars, let us think how great God is! Yet He cares for the little birds, and loves little children.[6]

Questions

- How many different sorts of things grow out of the ground?
- Tell me the names of some trees.
- Tell me the names of some vegetables.
- Tell me the names of some flowers.
- What bright things did God put in the sky?
- How many stars are there?

God is wise

A verse from the Bible for you to learn

He telleth the number of the stars; He calleth them all by their names. Ps. 147:4.

---

[2] 'Upholding all things by the word of His power.' Heb. 1:3.

[3] 'He appointed the moon for seasons: the sun knoweth his going down. Thou makest darkness, and it is night. . . . Man goeth forth unto his work, and to his labour until the evening.' Ps. 104:19, 20, 23.

[4] 'As the host of heaven cannot be numbered.' Jer. 33:22.

[5] 'Behold who hath created these things, that bringeth out their host by number: He calleth them all by names, by the greatness of His might.' Isa. 40:26.

[6] 'When I consider Thy heavens, the work of Thy fingers, the moon and the stars, which Thou hast ordained; what is man, that Thou art mindful of him?' Ps. 8:3, 4.

Lesson 9

The World

Part 3 — Genesis 1:20-25

God had made many things; but none of these things was alive. At last He made some living things. He spoke, and the water was filled with fish, more than could be counted.

Some were very small, and some were very large.[1] Have you heard about the huge whales? It is a fish as long as a church. Fish are cold; they have no feet; and they cannot sing or speak. God made some creatures more beautiful than fish. They fly about in the air. The birds perched on the trees and sang among the branches.[2]

Birds have wings, and are covered with feathers of all colours. The robin has a red breast, the goldfinch has some yellow feathers, and the jay some blue ones. But the peacock is the most beautiful of birds;[3] it has a little tuft on its head and a long train that sweeps behind; sometimes it spreads out its feathers, and they look like a large fan. The thrush, the blackbird and the linnet can sing sweetly, but there is one bird that can sing more sweetly still. It is the nightingale. At night, when all the other birds have left off singing, the nightingale may be heard in the woods.

Some birds swim on the water, such as geese and ducks and the beautiful swans with their long necks and feathers white like the snow. Some birds are very tall. The ostrich is as tall as a man. It cannot fly like other birds, but it can run very fast indeed.

---

[1] 'This great and wide sea, wherein are things creeping innumerable, both small and great beasts.' Ps. 104:25.

[2] 'The fowls of the heaven, which sing among the branches.' Ps. 104:12.

[3] 'Gavest thou the goodly wings unto the peacocks?' Job 39:13.

The eagle builds its nest in a very high place.[4] Its wings are very strong, and it can fly as high as the clouds.[5] The gentlest of the birds is the dove. It cannot sing, but it sits alone and moans softly, as if it was sad.[6] I cannot tell you the names of all the birds, but you can think of the names of some other kinds.

There is another sort of living creature, called insects. God made them come out of the earth, not out of the water like fishes. Insects such as ants are small, and creep on the earth. Some insects, such as bees and butterflies, can also fly. The bee sucks the juice of flowers, and makes wax and honey. How beautiful are the wings of a butterfly! They are covered with little feathers, too small to be seen. All the insects were good and pretty when God made them.

At last God made the animals. They were made from the earth when God spoke. Animals walk on the earth; most of them have four legs. You know the names of many sorts of animals. Sheep and cows, dogs and cats, are animals. But there are many other sorts: the squirrel that jumps from branch to branch, the rabbit that lives in a hole under the ground, and the goat that climbs the high hills; the stag with his beautiful horns, the lion with his yellow hair, and the tiger whose skin is marked with stripes. The elephant is the largest of the beasts, the lion is the strongest, the dog is the most sensible, the stag is the most beautiful, but the lamb is the gentlest. The dove is the gentlest of the birds, and the lamb is the gentlest of the animals.

Now God had filled the world with living creatures, and they were all good: even lions and tigers were good and harmless. I have told you of four sorts of living creatures:

---

[4] 'Doth the eagle mount up at thy command, and make her nest on high?' Job 39:27.

[5] 'They that wait upon the Lord shall renew their strength; they shall mount up with wings as eagles.' Isa. 40:31.

[6] 'They that escape of them shall escape, and shall be on the mountains like doves of the valleys, all of them mourning every one for his iniquity.' Ezek. 7:16.

1. Fishes.
2. Birds.
3. Insects.
4. Animals.

All these creatures have bodies, but they do not have souls like you. They can move and breathe. God feeds them every day, and keeps them alive.[7] The Lord is good to them all.

When God first clothed the earth with green,
And sprinkled it with flowers,
There was no living creature seen
Within its pleasant bowers.

Soon by His word God filled the earth,
And waters underneath,
With things above the plants in worth,
That feel and move and breathe.

The fishes, covered o'er with scales,
In ocean swiftly glide;
With their vast tails the wondrous whales
Scatter the waters wide.

The birds among the branches sing,
And chief the nightingale;
The peacock shines with painted wing,
The dove does softly wail.

Insects with humming fill the air,
And sparkle in the sun;
The butterfly by colours fair
Surpasses every one.

---

[7] 'These wait all upon Thee; that thou mayest give them their meat in due season.' Ps. 104:27.

The beasts tread firmly on the ground;
The goat has nimble feet;
The stag's with branching antlers crowned;
The lamb's most soft and sweet.

Pleasure the whole creation fills;
They leap, they swim, they fly;
They skim the plains, they climb the hills,
Or in the valleys lie.

In all the woods no sound of strife,
Or piteous moans arise;
None takes away his fellow's life,
And none expiring lies.

These happy days, alas! are past,
And death has entered here;
Why did they not for ever last?
And when did death appear?

Questions

- How many sorts of living things did God make?
- Tell me the names of some kinds of fish.
- Tell me the names of some birds.
- Tell me the names of some insects.
- Tell me the names of some animals.

God is kind to birds and beasts

A verse from the Bible for you to learn

He giveth to the beast his food, and to the young ravens which cry. Ps. 147:9.

Lesson 10

Adam and Eve

Genesis 1:26-2:25

Now I shall tell you of the last thing God made. God took some of the dust of the ground, and made the body of a man. Then He breathed on it and gave it a soul, so that the man could understand about God. This first man whom God made was called Adam. Adam was good; he did nothing bad. [1] Adam loved God very much.

God put him in a very pretty garden, full of trees covered with fruit. This garden was called the garden of Eden. God showed Adam all the beasts and birds, and let Adam give them whatever names he wanted. He said to Adam, 'I give you all the fishes and insects and birds and beasts. You are their master.' So Adam was king over all things on the earth.

God said to Adam, 'You may eat of the fruit that grows on the trees in the garden.' Still God did not let him be idle, but told him to take care of the garden. You see how very kind God was to Adam.

But Adam had no friend to be with him; for the beasts and birds could not talk to Adam. Then God said He would make a woman to be a friend to Adam. So God made Adam fall fast asleep. God took a piece of bone and flesh out of his side, and made it into a woman. When Adam woke, he saw her. He knew that she was made of his flesh and bones, and he loved her very much. Her name was 'woman,' and afterwards her name was Eve.

You have heard of all the things God made. They were all beautiful, and all the living things were happy. There was no pain and no crying and no sin in all the world.

---

[1] 'God hath made man upright.' Eccles. 7:29.

God had been six days in making the world. And when He had finished it, He rested on the seventh day. He made no more things.

The angels saw the world that God had made. They were pleased; they sang a sweet song of praise to God.[2] Jesus Christ, the Son of God, was pleased, for He loved Adam and Eve.[3]

How do I know about the world being made? Because it is written in the Bible, which is God's own book.

Let us count over all the things that God made.

1. Light.
2. Air.
3. Clouds.
4. Sea.
5. Dry land.
6. Things that grow out of the earth.
7. Sun, moon and stars.
8. Living creatures.

Questions

- What was the last thing that God made?
- How did God make Adam?
- Where did God put Adam?
- What did God give him?
- Why did God make Eve?
- How did He make her?
- How many days did God take to make the world?
- Tell me the names of all the things God made.

---

[2] 'Where wast thou when I laid the foundations of the earth? . . . When the morning stars sang together, and all the sons of God shouted for joy?' Job 38:4, 7.

[3] 'Rejoicing in the habitable part of His earth; and My delights were with the sons of men.' Prov. 8:31.

How beautiful the world was at first

A verse from the Bible for you to learn

And God saw everything that He had made, and, behold, it was very good. Gen. 1:31.

LESSON 11

The First Sin

GENESIS 3

ADAM and Eve were very happy in the garden of Eden. They talked to each other and walked together. They never quarrelled, but they praised God for all His kindness to them. God used to talk with them sometimes. They were pleased to hear His voice, for they were not afraid of Him.

There was one thing that God had told them not to do. There was a tree in the middle of the garden. Some beautiful fruit grew on it; but God said to Adam and Eve, 'You must not eat of the fruit of that tree. If you eat of it, you shall die.'

Adam and Eve liked to obey God, and they did not wish to eat of this fruit.

You know that the wicked angel, Satan, hates God, and he hated Adam and Eve.[1] He wished to make them bad, so that they might go to hell and be burned in his fire. He thought he would ask them to eat of that fruit. He went into the garden and spoke through a serpent.[2]

---

[1] 'Love is of God; and every one that loveth is born of God, and knoweth God.' 1 John 4:7.

[2] 'That old serpent, called the Devil, and Satan, which deceiveth the whole world.' Rev. 12:9.

He saw Eve alone near the tree. He said to her, 'Why do you not eat of this fruit?'

Eve answered, 'No, I will not; we must not eat of that fruit. If we do, God has said we shall die.'

Then the serpent said, 'You shall not die; the fruit will make you wise.'

Eve looked at the fruit, and thought it was nice and pretty. She picked some and ate it. Then she gave some to Adam, and he ate it. It was very wicked of them to eat this fruit. Now they were wicked, and did not love God.[3]

Soon they heard God speaking in the garden. They were frightened, and they went to hide among the trees. But God saw them, for He can see everywhere.

So God said, 'Adam, where art thou?' Then Adam and Eve came from under the trees.

God said to Adam, 'Have you eaten the fruit that I told you not to eat?'

And Adam said, 'It was this woman who asked me to eat some.'

And God said to Eve, 'What is this that thou hast done?'

And Eve said, 'The serpent asked me to eat.'

God was very angry with the serpent, and said he should be punished for ever and ever.[4]

God said to Adam and Eve, 'You shall die. I made your bodies of dust, and they will turn to dust again.'

God would not let them stay in the nice garden. He made them go out. He would not let them come back. He told one of His bright angels to stand before the gate with a sword of fire, and to keep Adam and Eve out of the garden.

Near Eden's land, in days gone by,
A lovely garden stood;
The trees were pleasant to the eye;
The fruit was good for food.

---

[3] 'By one man's disobedience many were made sinners.' Rom. 5:19.
[4] 'It shall bruise thy head.' Gen. 3:15.

Two holy creatures spent their days
Within that garden fair:
In love they dwelt; they sang God's praise,
And humbly knelt in prayer.

In that sweet land one tree was placed,
Their faithful love to try.
'That fruit,' God said, 'you shall not taste;
Who eats shall surely die.'

O why did Eve to Satan's lies
So readily attend?
Upon the fruit why fix her eyes,
Then pluck it with her hand?

No more shall Eve or Adam stay
Within that garden fair;
An angel stands to guard the way,
That none may enter there.

Questions

- What did God tell Adam and Eve not to do?
- Who asked Eve to eat the fruit?
- Why did he ask her?
- What lie did the serpent tell to Eve?
- Were Adam and Eve good after they had eaten the fruit?
- Why did they hide under the trees?
- What did God say should be done to Adam and Eve, to punish them?
- Who drove them out of the garden?

How sin came into the world

A verse from the Bible for you to learn

By one man sin entered into the world. Rom. 5:12.

LESSON 12

The Son of God

GENESIS 3:14-24

I AM sure you are very sorry to hear that Adam and Eve were turned out of the garden? It was not so pleasant outside the garden. Many, many weeds and thistles now grew outside; but in the garden there were only pretty flowers and sweet fruits.

Adam was forced to dig the ground till he was hot and tired, for he could not always find fruit on the trees. Now Adam felt pain in his body sometimes. His hair became grey, and at last he was quite old. Eve was very often sick and weak, and tears ran down her cheeks.

Poor Adam and Eve! If they had obeyed God they would have been happy for ever.

Adam and Eve knew that they must die at last. God gave them some little children, and Adam and Eve knew that their children must die too. God had told them that their bodies were made of dust, and that they must turn to dust again.

But there was something more sad still. They were now wicked. They did not love to praise God, as they once had done, but they liked doing many bad things.[1] They were now like Satan. So Satan hoped that, when their bodies would be put into the ground, their spirits would be with him, for Satan knew that wicked people cannot live with God in heaven.[2]

And they would have gone to hell, and all their children too, if God had not taken pity on them. God, who is very kind, had found a way to save them.

---

[1] 'The carnal mind is enmity against God: for it is not subject to the law of God, neither indeed can be.' Rom. 8:7.

[2] 'And the Lord said, Simon, Simon, behold, Satan hath desired to have you.' Luke 22:31. The constant efforts of Satan to tempt man to commit sin show that he is aware of the destructive nature of sin, as it is undeniable that he desires to destroy man.

God had said to His Son, a long, long while before then, 'Adam and Eve and all their children must go to hell for their wickedness, unless Thou wilt die.[3] My beloved Son, I will send Thee. Thou shalt have a body. Thou shalt go and live in the world and Thou shalt obey Me. And Thou shalt take the place of very many men and women and children and die instead of them.'[4]

The Son said to His Father, 'I will come.' He would do all that the Father wanted Him to do. He said, It is My delight to obey Thee.'[5] So the Son promised to come into this world to die.

How kind it was of the Father to send His dear Son, whom He loved so very much![6] How kind it was of the Son to come from His throne of light and His bright angels, and to take a body and to die![7]

You know that we are some of Adam's children's children. It was for such people that Jesus came to die. We are wicked, and we should go to hell, if Jesus had not promised to die for such people.[8] We ought to love the Father and the Son, because They had pity on sinners.

Let us praise God with the angels,[9] and say,

'We thank Thee, O Father, for Thy tender love in giving Thine only Son.

'We thank Thee, O Son, for Thy tender love in coming down to bleed and die.'

---

[3] 'Herein is love, not that we loved God, but that He loved us, and sent His Son to be the propitiation for our sins.' 1 John 4:10. 'Who verily was foreordained before the foundation of the world.' 1 Pet. 1:20.

[4] 'I have kept My Father's commandments, and abide in His love.' John 15:10.

[5] 'Then said I, Lo, I come . . . I delight to do Thy will, O My God: yea, Thy law is within My heart.' Ps. 40:7, 8.

[6] 'Thou lovedst Me before the foundation of the world.' John 17:24.

[7] 'The glory which I had with Thee before the world was.' John 17:5.

[8] 'As in Adam all die, even so in Christ shall all be made alive.' 1 Cor. 15:22.

[9] 'I heard the voice of many angels . . . saying with a loud voice, Worthy is the Lamb that was slain. . . . And every creature . . . heard I saying Blessing, and honour, and glory, and power, be unto Him that sitteth upon the throne, and unto the Lamb for ever and ever.' Rev. 5:11-13.

The Father waited a long while before He sent His Son down to be a man. All the time the Son waited in heaven, He thought of what He promised to do.[10] But He would not go and be a man till His Father was pleased to send Him.[11]

Adam has sinned, and on the ground
Shall thorns and thistles grow.
His body lie in dust; his soul,
Ah, whither shall it go?

Shall one who dared to disobey,
With God for ever dwell?
When angels sinned God did not spare,
But cast them down to hell.

Yet long before the world was made
Our God contrived a plan,
By which his sinful soul to save,
And pardon guilty man.

The Father said His Son should die,
The Son replied, 'I will.
A feeble body I will take;
This body men shall kill.'

Father, how great Thy love to man,
To send Thy Son from high!
How great Thy love, O glorious Son,
To come, and bleed, and die!

---

[10] Visits of the Son of God to man, in anticipation of his sacrifice, are recorded often in the Old Testament. His visit to Abraham, in Gen. 18; to Jacob, Gen. 32; to Moses in the bush, Exod. 3; to Joshua, Josh. 5; to Isaiah, Isa. 6 compared with John 12:41. The Son of God is evidently referred to in the following passage: 'He bare them, and carried them all the days of old.' Isa. 63:9.

[11] 'When the fulness of the time was come, God sent forth His Son.' Gal. 4:4.

Questions

- Were Adam and Eve happy after they had eaten the fruit?
- Why not?
- Who took pity on them?
- What did God wish His Son to do for Adam?
- What did God's Son say to His Father, when He told Him to be a man so that He could die?
- Are we some of Adam's children?
- If Jesus did not die, where would Adam and Eve and all their children go when they died?
- Did Jesus come down into the world as soon as Adam became wicked?
- Did He wait a long while, or a little while?

God sent a Saviour

A verse from the Bible for you to learn

The Father sent the Son to be the Saviour of the world.
1 John 4:14.

LESSON 13

The Virgin Mary

LUKE 1:26-55

GOD told Adam and Eve that He would send His Son down some day to die for them. But Adam and Eve did not love God, for they were now wicked.

Could God make them good?

Yes, He could, for in heaven there is the Holy Spirit. And the Holy Spirit could come into them and make them good.

You know, my little children, we are wicked, and God can make us good by His Holy Spirit. If God puts His Holy Spirit in us, we shall not go to hell and live with Satan.[1]

I hope you will ask God to give you His Holy Spirit. Say to God, 'O give me Thy Holy Spirit to make me good!'

Adam had a great many children and grandchildren, and they had more children. At last the world was full of people — more people than you could count.

After Adam and Eve had been dead a long while, and when the world was full of people, God said to His Son, 'Now, My beloved Son, go down into the world.' But God chose that His Son should be a little baby at first. Everybody is a little baby at first.

God sent His Son to be the baby of a poor woman. This woman's name was Mary. Mary had no little children. She was a good woman and loved God. God's Holy Spirit was in her and made her meek and gentle.

One day an angel came to her. When Mary saw the bright angel she was frightened; but the angel said, 'Fear not, Mary; God loves you. He will send you a baby. That baby will be the Son of God. You shall call His name Jesus. He will come to save people from Satan.'

Mary was very surprised at what the angel said. She thought she was not good enough to have such a baby as the Lord Jesus.

When the angel went back to heaven, Mary sang a sweet song of praise to God for His goodness. Mary said, 'My soul praises God, and my spirit is glad because of my Saviour.' Mary called her baby her Saviour, for she knew that He would save her from hell.

---

[1] 'God hath from the beginning chosen you to salvation through sanctification of the Spirit and belief of the truth.' 2 Thess. 2:13.

Questions

- Did Adam and Eve know that God would send His Son to die for them?
- Could God make Adam and Eve good again?
- How could they be made good?
- What must you ask for, if you wish to be good?
- When did God send His Son down into the world?
- Whose little baby did God's Son choose to be?
- Who told her she would have a little baby?
- What name did the angel say she was to give her baby?
- What did Mary do when the angel went back to heaven?

Why Christ came

A verse from the Bible for you to learn

Christ Jesus came into the world to save sinners. 1 Tim 1:15.

LESSON 14

The Birth of Jesus

LUKE 2:1-7

MARY'S husband was called called Joseph. He was a good man, and very kind to Mary.

Now, before Mary's baby was born, a great king said that everybody must have their names written down.[1] So Mary and

---

[1] The word translated 'taxed' signifies 'enrolled'. A general census of the Roman empire was made at this time.

Joseph left their house and went on a long journey. At last they came to a town called Bethlehem.

But where could they sleep?

They went to an inn, and said, 'Do let us in. We have come from somewhere far away.'

But the man who kept the inn said, 'I have no room in my inn for you.'

What could poor Mary do? Must she sleep in the street?

No, the man let her sleep in the stable. So Mary and Joseph went into the stable. There were cows and asses in the stable.

While Mary was in the stable, God sent her the little baby He had promised her. She knew He was the Son of God, though He looked like other little babies.

She wrapped Him in some long clothes, called swaddling clothes. But she had no cradle for Him to sleep in, and she could not lay Him on the ground because the animals might stand on Him. So she put Him in the manger, and she sat by Him to take care of Him. How dearly Mary loved this sweet babe!

This baby did not have a bad heart as other babies have.[2] Jesus had no sin, but was meek and lowly. Yet other babies have cradles and soft pillows, while Jesus lay in a manger.

I will tell you a verse to say to your little baby brother or sister when you rock the cradle.

> Soft and easy is your cradle;
> Coarse and hard the Saviour lay,
> When His birth-place was a stable,
> And His softest bed was hay.

---

[2] 'That holy thing, which shall be born of thee.' Luke 1:35. 'Was in all points tempted like as we are, yet without sin.' Heb 4:15.

Questions

- What was the name of Mary's husband?
- Why did Mary and Joseph take a long journey?
- What town did they come to?
- Did they sleep in the inn at night?
- Why not?
- Where did they sleep?
- What baby was born while Mary was in the stable?
- Did Mary know it was the Son of God?
- Where did she lay her baby?
- What did she wrap Him in?
- Did Jesus look like other babies?
- Was His heart like other babies' hearts?

About Mary and the Lord Jesus

A verse from the Bible for you to learn

And she brought forth her firstborn Son, and wrapped Him in swaddling clothes, and laid Him in a manger. Luke 2:7.

LESSON 15

The Shepherds

LUKE 2:8-20

THERE were fields near Bethlehem. On the night when Jesus was born, some shepherds were sitting by their sheep in those fields. Why did they sit up at night? To keep their sheep from the wolves and lions which walk about at night. There are no wolves and lions where we live, but near Bethlehem there were some.

These shepherds saw a great light. A beautiful angel came from heaven. The poor shepherds were afraid; but the angel said, 'Fear not, I have good news to tell you. God has sent His own Son from heaven to save you from hell. He is a baby now, lying in a manger. Go to Bethlehem, and you will find Him.'

When the angel finished speaking, hundreds and hundreds of bright angels filled the sky, and began singing and praising God for having sent His Son to save many people.

At last the angels went back to heaven, and the shepherds were left alone.

Did they stay with their sheep?

No. They said, 'Let us go and see the Son of God.'

They ran to Bethlehem and went to the stable at the inn. There was a babe lying in the manger. Mary and Joseph were sitting beside it. The shepherds said, 'This is the Son of God. Angels have spoken to us tonight. They told us where to find Him.'

All the people in Bethlehem were very surprised when the shepherds told them about the angels and the Son of God.

Blessed Babe! What glorious features,
Spotless fair, divinely bright!
Must He dwell with brutish creatures?
How could angels bear the sight?

Was there nothing but a manger
Wretched sinners could afford,
To receive the heavenly stranger?
Did they thus affront the Lord?

See the kinder shepherds round Him,
Telling wonders from the sky.
Where they sought Him, there they found Him,
With His virgin mother by.

Questions

- Who were in the fields near Bethlehem the night Jesus was born?
- Why did the shepherds sit up at night?
- What did they see in the sky?
- What did the angels tell them?
- Who sang the songs in the sky?
- When the angels went away, where did the shepherds go?
- Did the shepherds tell people what they had seen?

What the shepherds did

A verse from the Bible for you to learn

And they came with haste, and found Mary, and Joseph, and the babe lying in a manger. Luke 2:16.

LESSON 16

The Wise Men

MATTHEW 2

THERE were some wise and rich men who lived a long way from Bethlehem. They knew that God had sent His Son to be a babe, but they did not know where to find Him. So God put a beautiful star in the sky, and God made it move towards the place where Jesus was.

So the wise men left their houses, and set out on a long journey, but first they said, 'Let us bring some presents for the Son of God, for He is a king.'

They took some gold, and some sweet-smelling stuff (to burn). They looked at the star as they went. At last it stopped over a house in Bethlehem. The wise men were very glad indeed. They longed to see the Son of God.

They went in, and there they saw Mary and her child Jesus. They fell down and began to praise Him, and to call Him the Son of God and the King. They took out their presents, and gave them to Him. Mary was poor, but now she had some money to buy things for her little baby.

Lo, travellers enter Bethlehem's gate,
Arrived from some far-distant land;
They seem to be of high estate
And hold rich presents in their hand.

They swiftly pass from street to street,
Nor need they fear to go astray,
Nor need they ask the men they meet
To guide them in their unknown way.

For see where shines a beauteous star;
On it they fix their joyful eyes:
That heavenly guide has led them far,
And now it lightens Bethlehem's skies.

But, lo, it stops, its course is done;
On Mary's roof it sheds a light.
Enter, there dwells God's blessed Son.
Enter, enjoy the glorious sight.

But where is He, the Lord of all,
Who made the heavens and earth and seas?
Behold Him there, an infant small,
Lying upon His mother's knees!

Their Lord full well the strangers know,
And humbly worship at His feet,
Joyful their golden treasures show,
And burn their precious spices sweet.

O happy they who knelt that day
Before the lovely infant's face,
And who believed, though born a child,
That He was Lord of every place!

And shall not I be happy too,
If, though His face I never saw,
I feel for Him affection true,
And still obey His holy law?

No gold nor spices need I give,
To show my Lord how much I love;
But I may serve Him while I live,
And thus my warm affection prove.

Questions

- Who came from far away to see Jesus?
- Who told them that God had sent His Son to be a baby?
- How did they find the way to Bethlehem?
- What did they bring with them?
- Where did the star stop?
- What did the wise men do when they saw Jesus?

The Great King

A verse from the Bible for you to learn

God is the King of all the earth: sing ye praises. Ps:47:7.

Lesson 17

King Herod

Matthew 2, Luke 2:51, 52

There was a very wicked king called Herod. He lived not very far from Bethlehem. He heard that a babe was born in Bethlehem, and that some people said that the babe was a king.

Now Herod did not like to think that there might be any other king besides himself. Herod did not even like to think that the Son of God should be king. So Herod said, 'I will kill this babe that is called a king.'

Herod knew that this babe was in Bethlehem; but there were many babes in Bethlehem, and Herod did not know which was the babe that was called a king.

Some people knew which it was, but they loved Jesus and they would not tell Herod. A very wicked thought came into Herod's mind. He said to himself, 'I will kill all the babes in Bethlehem.' Do you think God would let Herod kill His Son?

No. God knew what Herod meant to do. God sent one of His bright angels to speak to Joseph when he was asleep.

The angel said, 'A wicked king wants to kill the baby. Get up, Joseph; take Mary and the baby far away.'

So Joseph got up quickly. He took his ass. He put Mary on it, and she held the baby. Perhaps it was dark when they set off; nobody saw them go.

The next morning some men came with swords. Herod had sent them. They came to kill all the babies. They opened every door and asked, 'Is there a baby here?' Then they snatched it from its mother and killed it, and the poor mother cried bitterly.

If you walked down the streets, you would have heard nothing but women weeping and crying out, 'My lovely babe is dead. I shall never see it more!'

Was Jesus killed?

No: He was now far away. His Father, God, had sent Him away. Herod could not kill Him, for God would not let Him die so soon.

At last king Herod died. Then God sent an angel to speak to Joseph when he was asleep. The angel said, 'Joseph, go back to your own country. Herod is dead.'

So Joseph took the ass, and Mary, and the sweet child, Jesus, and they all came back to their own country.

Joseph was a carpenter. Jesus lived with Joseph and Mary and obeyed them. He was a wise child, and loved to think of God. God His Father loved Him, and everybody loved Him, because He was so meek and kind.

Questions

- Who wanted to kill Jesus when He was a baby?
- Were there many babies in Bethlehem?
- Did King Herod know which baby was the Son of God?
- Who did Herod want to kill?
- Did he kill Jesus?
- Why not?
- Who told Joseph to take Jesus far away?
- Did Herod know that Jesus had gone away?
- Did Herod think he had killed Jesus?
- Who did Herod send to kill the babies in Bethlehem?
- Did Jesus ever come back to His own country?
- Who told Joseph to take Jesus back to His country?
- Why was it safe for Jesus to come back to His own country?
- What was Joseph's work?
- Did the people love Jesus when He was a child?
- Why did they love Him?

God can help us always

A verse from the Bible for you to learn

My help cometh from the Lord, which made heaven and earth. Ps. 121:2.

Lesson 18

The Temptation

Matthew 4:1-11

At last Jesus grew up to be a man. He knew that He must go from place to place and teach people about God.

But first He went alone, led by the Spirit, into a place called a wilderness. He had no house to sleep in there, no friend to speak to and no food to eat. In the night it was cold, in the day very hot.

There were no men, but there were lions, wolves, and bears.[1] At night they roared and howled, but Jesus trusted in His Father.

He ate nothing for forty days and forty nights. God kept Him alive. When Jesus was alone, He spoke in His heart to His dear Father.[2]

At last some one came and spoke to Him.

Who was it?

---

1 'And (He) was with the wild beasts.' Mark 1:13.

2 'Yet I am not alone, because the Father is with Me.' John 16:32.

Not a man, not a bright angel, not God; it was Satan. I do not know what he looked like. He came to tempt Jesus to do wicked things. He came to tempt Jesus not to obey God His Father.

Satan knew that Jesus was hungry. He said to Jesus, 'Turn these stones into bread!' But Jesus would not do that, for God had promised to feed Him Himself.

After that, Satan took Jesus to the top of a great building, that was much higher than a church. It is frightening to be at the top of a very high place; it makes one tremble to look down from the top.

Satan said to Jesus, 'Throw Thyself down from this place; Thy Father will send His angels to keep Thee from being hurt, for He has promised to take care of Thee.'

Would Jesus have done right, if He had thrown Himself down? No. Jesus knew that His Father would be displeased if He threw Himself down; and Jesus always did the things that pleased His Father.

Then Satan took Jesus to the top of a very high hill. He showed Him the most beautiful things in the world: trees and gardens, houses and ships, and fine clothes and feasts. He said, 'Look at these fine things.' Satan promised to give them all to Jesus. He would give Jesus the whole world. All Jesus had to do was to kneel down and worship Satan. But Jesus said, 'I will pray to My Father, and not to you.'

Jesus loved His Father better than all the things in the world. Adam and Eve listened to Satan and disobeyed God, but Jesus did everything His Father told Him. Adam was disobedient; Jesus was obedient.

Then Satan went away; and angels came from heaven and fed Jesus.

Satan goes about, trying to make children do bad things. A lion could only eat your body, but Satan wants to have your soul and body in hell. Satan hates you. He is your enemy. But God is stronger than Satan.[3] Say to God, 'Keep me from doing what Satan tells me to do,' and God will keep you.

---

[3] 'Greater is He that is in you, than he that is in the world.' 1 John 4:4.

Upon that mountain's height
Two mighty princes stand:
Jesus the prince of light,
Satan at His right hand.
Below them lies the prospect fair
Of all this earth holds rich or rare.

Tables are seen around,
Spread with delicious meats;
Gardens where fruits abound,
And thousand tempting sweets;
Silver and gold and precious stones,
Chariots and palaces and thrones.

Satan did once prevail
On Eve to disobey;
And now why should he fail
To tempt the Lord astray?
For Eve abundant food possessed,
While Christ with hunger is distressed.

In vain the tempter tries
The Saviour to deceive,
For Jesus came from heaven
Our miseries to relieve:
His Father dear He sought to please,
Nor wished for earthly joy and ease.

He had seen brighter things,
And sweeter joys had known,
Where angels touch the strings
Around His Father's throne;
And shall He from that throne descend,
Before the evil one to bend?

No, He will hunger bear,
And suffer sharpest pain,
Till God shall hear His prayer,

And His weak life sustain.
And, lo, ashamed the tempter flies,
And angels feed Him from the skies.

Full oft does Satan try
To draw my steps aside;
Now bids me tell a lie,
My faults from all to hide;
And tempts me soon to sin again,
That I new pleasure may obtain.

Whenever I consent
To walk in Satan's ways
It is as though I bent
My knee before his face.
And what reward will Satan give?
In his own hell with him to live.

How shall my feeble heart
Be kept from Satan's power?
O Lord, Thy strength impart
In every tempted hour,
That I may sinful joys refuse,
And Thy sweet service ever choose.

Questions

- When Jesus grew to be a man, where did He go by Himself?
- Were there animals in the wilderness?
- How many days was Jesus there?
- What did He eat?
- Who came to Him at last?
- Why did Satan come?
- What did Satan ask Jesus to do first?
- Why would Jesus not turn the stones into bread?

- What did Satan ask Jesus to do when he had taken Him to the top of a high building?
- Why would Jesus not throw Himself down?
- What did Satan show Jesus from the top of a hill?
- What did Satan say Jesus must do, if He would have all these fine things?
- Would Jesus do this?
- Who fed Jesus after Satan went away?
- What harm does Satan want to do to children and to everyone?

The devil is cruel

A verse from the Bible for you to learn

The devil, as a roaring lion, walketh about, seeking whom he may devour. 1 Pet. 5:8.

Lesson 19

The Twelve Disciples

Mark 1:16-20

When Jesus was a man, He began to teach people about His Father. Jesus used to preach.

Where did He preach?

Sometimes He preached to people in a place like a church. Sometimes He preached in the fields. Sometimes He sat on the top of a hill and preached. And sometimes He sat in a ship, and the people stood by the edge of the water to hear Him.

Jesus did not always live in the same place. He used to walk about from one place to another.

Did Jesus walk about alone?

No. He had twelve friends with Him. He called them His twelve disciples.

How many are twelve?

Let us count the little children in this room. Here are twelve. Jesus had just as many disciples. One was called Peter, and another was called John, and another James, and another Thomas. But I will not tell you the names of them all; you would not remember them all.

Peter was a fisherman. He had a little ship, and he used to catch fish, sometimes even at night. James and John had another little ship, and they used to catch fish too.

One day Jesus passed by their ships. He saw Peter and his brother Andrew throwing a net into the sea to catch fish. Jesus said to them, 'Come with Me.' And Peter and Andrew left their nets and their ships and went with Jesus.

Jesus went a little farther, and He saw James and John sitting in their ship, mending their nets because they were torn. Jesus said to them, 'Come with Me'. They left their nets and went with Jesus. Jesus called whatever people He wanted to come with Him.

Shall I tell you why Jesus chose to have twelve friends always with Him? What do you think was the reason?

Jesus wished to teach them about God His Father,[1] so that they might teach other people about Him.[2] They liked being with Jesus, and listening to His words.[3] Would you have liked to be always with Jesus?

---

[1] Christ said in prayer to His Father, 'I have manifested Thy name unto the men which Thou gavest Me out of the world.' John 17:6.

[2] 'And He ordained twelve, that they should be with Him and that He might send them forth to preach.' Mark 3:14.

[3] 'Then said Jesus unto the twelve, Will ye also go away? Then Simon Peter answered Him, Lord, to whom shall we go? Thou hast the words of eternal life.' John 6:67, 68.

When Jesus was alone with His disciples, He used to tell them secrets about God[4] and heaven. They loved Him very much indeed;[5] they called Him Master and Lord.[6] Jesus loved them still more than they loved Him,[7] and He called them His friends.[8]

Jesus used to give them part of His things. But Jesus had no house to live in,[9] and He had very little money.[10] Sometimes Jesus and His friends were very tired after walking for a long time,[11] and sometimes they were very hungry and thirsty.[12] But kind people often asked them to come into their houses, and gave them food.[13] Other people laughed at Jesus, and called Him names.[14]

Were the disciples good?

They were bad, like us; but Jesus put His Spirit into them, and made them better.[15] The disciples were not completely good, like Jesus; they sometimes quarrelled with each other,[16] and sometimes they were unkind to poor people.[17]

---

[4] 'When they were alone, He expounded all things to His disciples.' Mark 4:34.

[5] 'The Father Himself loveth you, because ye have loved Me.' John 16:27.

[6] 'Ye call Me Master, and Lord.' John 13:13.

[7] 'As the Father hath loved Me, so have I loved you.' John 15:9.

[8] 'I have called you friends.' John 15:15.

[9] 'The Son of Man hath not where to lay His head.' Luke 9:58.

[10] Jesus having recourse to a miracle to obtain money to pay tribute, testifies to His poverty; and His sharing it with Peter ('Give unto them for Me and thee') shows that He shared His supplies with His disciples. Matt. 17:24-27.

[11] 'Jesus, therefore, being wearied with His journey, sat thus on the well.' John 4:6.

[12] 'His disciples were an hungered, and began to pluck the ears of corn.' Matt. 12:1.

[13] 'A certain woman named Martha received Him into her house.' Luke 10:38. 'There they made Him a supper.' John 12:2.

[14] 'Say we are not well that Thou art a Samaritan, and hast a devil?' John 8:48.

[15] 'Now ye are clean through the word which I have spoken unto you.' John 15:3.

[16] 'And there was also a strife among them, which of them should be accounted the greatest.' Luke 22:24.

[17] Witness their conduct to the woman of Canaan. Matt. 15:23.

How happy they who shared the bread
Of Jesus here below!
From place to place He travelled,
And they with Him did go.

They heard Him preach from hills and ships
Of things to men unknown;
But sweeter words dropped from His lips
When they were all alone.

For then He would the things explain
They could not understand,
That heavenly wisdom they might gain,
And teach it through the land.

Questions

- Where did Jesus preach?
- How many disciples did Jesus have?
- Did they ever quarrel?
- Can you tell me the names of some of them?
- What was Peter doing when Jesus told him to come with Him?
- What were James and John doing when Jesus called them?
- Why did Jesus choose to have some friends with Him?
- What did they call Jesus?
- What did He call them?
- Did they love Jesus?
- Why did they like being with Him?
- Did Jesus give them money or fine things?
- Why were the disciples good?

Christ was very poor

A verse from the Bible for you to learn

Foxes have holes, and birds of the air have nests; but the Son of man hath not where to lay His head. Luke 9:58.

LESSON 20

The First Miracle

JOHN 2:1-11

I TOLD you that some people used to ask Jesus to come into their houses. I shall now tell you about such a man. This man gave a feast, and Jesus came to the feast. Mary, Jesus' mother, came, and the disciples came. There were many other people at the feast.

There was some wine for the people to drink, but there was so little that very soon it was all finished. Jesus knew that the wine was finished. Could Jesus not give the people more wine?

Yes. He made the world and all things in it.

There were some large stone jars in the house. Jesus said to the servants, 'Fill the jars with water,' and they filled them to the very top.

Then Jesus said, 'Take some, and give it to the man in charge of the feast.' The servants did so; but Jesus had turned the water into wine.

When the man had tasted it, he said, 'What nice wine this is! Where did it come from?'

The servants told him how Jesus had said to them to fill the jars with water. Then all the people at the feast knew that Jesus had turned the water into wine. This was the first wonder that Jesus did; it was called a miracle.

Why did Jesus do miracles?

To show people that He was the Son of God. The disciples now felt quite sure that Jesus was the Son of God.

Questions

- When Jesus was at the feast, what was finished very soon?
- How did Jesus make more wine?
- What was the first miracle Jesus did?

What the Father gave to the Son

A verse from the Bible for you to learn

The Father loveth the Son, and hath given all things into His hand. John 3:35.

LESSON 21

Several Miracles

LUKE 6:11-16

AFTER Jesus had turned the water into wine, he did many other wonders. He made blind people see and deaf people hear. He made dumb people speak and lame people walk.

When Jesus came to a place, all the sick people crowded round Him. Jesus did not send them away because they disturbed Him, but He cured them all. Yes, every one of them. [1]

---

[1] 'He laid his hands on every one of them, and healed them.' Luke 4:40.

This was the way in which Jesus cured one blind man. He said, 'See!' And the man could see at that moment.[2]

This was the way in which He cured a man who was deaf and dumb. Jesus put His fingers into his ears and touched his tongue. He looked up to His Father in heaven and said 'Be opened!' And immediately the string of his tongue was loosed, and he could speak plainly.[3]

Once Jesus saw a poor sick man lying on a bed. Jesus said to him, 'Would you like to be made well?' The poor man said he wished very much to be made well. Then Jesus said, 'Get up; carry your bed and walk.' When the man tried to get up, he found that he could; for Jesus gave him strength.[4]

One day Jesus was in a place like a church. When He was preaching, He saw a poor woman whose back was so bent that she could not lift up her head. Jesus said, 'Woman, I have made you well.' Then Jesus touched her with His hands, and her back grew straight, and she began to praise God.[5]

Sometimes Jesus made dead people alive again. That was even more wonderful than making sick people well.

Once Jesus was walking on the road. Many people were walking after Him, for people liked to see Him do wonders and to hear Him talk. They met some men carrying a dead man to put him in the ground.

A poor woman came after them, crying very much. She was the mother of the dead man. He was her only son. Jesus was very sorry to see her crying. He came up to her and said: 'Do not cry.' Then He touched the coffin. There was no top to it and the dead man was lying in it.

Jesus said, 'Get up, young man!' He sat up and began to speak. Then Jesus said to his mother, 'Here is your son.'

All the people were surprised, and said, 'This must be the Son of God. He can make dead people live again.'

---

[2] Luke 18:42.

[3] Mark 7:32-35.

[4] John 5:5-9.

[5] Luke 13:11-13.

Questions

- Why did sick and blind people come to Jesus?
- How did He cure one blind man?
- How did He cure a deaf and dumb man?
- What did He say to a man who was ill in bed?
- What did He say to the woman whose back was bent?
- What could Jesus do that was more wonderful than making sick people well?
- When Jesus was walking in the road, what did He see being carried by some men?
- Who was crying very much because the man was dead?
- What did Jesus say to the dead man?
- What did the man do?
- What did the people say when they saw the dead man come to life?

The wonders that Jesus did

A verse from the Bible for you to learn

He maketh both the deaf to hear, and the dumb to speak.
Mark 7:37.

LESSON 22

The Sinner and Simon

LUKE 7:36-50

WHY did Jesus come into the world?
To save people from hell.
But why did God say that people must go to hell?
Because everybody was bad.

Jesus can forgive people their badness, and make them good. But those whom Jesus forgives, He also makes them sorry for their sins. I will tell you about a proud man who was not sorry, and of a poor woman who was sorry.

A rich proud man asked Jesus to come and dine with him. Why did he ask Jesus? He did not love Him; he only asked Him so that he might hear Him talk. Yet Jesus said He would come.

The proud man did not treat Jesus very kindly. He gave Him no water to wash His feet, He put no nice-smelling ointment on them, he gave Jesus no kiss.

A poor woman, who had been very wicked, saw Jesus go into the rich man's house. She came up behind Jesus and began to cry for all her sins. She knew Jesus could forgive her, and she loved Jesus.

She had brought a box of ointment with her. She stooped down and her tears fell upon Jesus' feet, and with her tears she washed them. She wiped them with her long hair. Then she poured the nice ointment on them and kissed them.

The rich man looked at the woman very angrily; he knew she had been very wicked, and he was angry at seeing Jesus so kind to her.

But Jesus said to the proud man, 'This woman has been very wicked, but I have forgiven her, and she loves Me very much. She loves Me a great deal more than you do. You gave Me no water for My feet, but she has washed My feet with her tears. You gave Me no kiss, but she has kissed My feet ever since I came in. You gave Me no ointment, but she has poured very sweet ointment upon My feet.'

Then Jesus spoke kindly to the woman, and said to her, 'Your sins are forgiven. Your faith has saved you.' So Jesus comforted this poor woman, but the proud man and his friends grew still more angry.

Jesus will forgive your sins if you if you ask Him;[1] but if you think yourself good, He will not forgive you. Jesus cannot bear

---

[1] 'If we confess our sins, He is faithful and just to forgive us our sins.' 1 John 1:9.

proud people.[2] Though you are only a little child, you have done many wrong things; and you do not deserve to go to heaven. Oh, I hope Jesus will forgive you! I hope the Holy Spirit will come into your heart and make you feel very sorry for your sins. Then you will love Him, as this poor woman did.

O tell me who is standing there
With weeping eyes and flowing hair,
And box of ointment sweet.
Now on the ground she's bending low;
Her tears yet fast and faster flow;
They fall on Jesus' feet.

To her dear Lord such love she bears,
His feet she washes with her tears,
And wipes them with her hair;
And then, with pious tenderness,
Fond kisses ceases not to press,
And pours the ointment rare.

Ah she, whose love is now so strong,
Has wandered far, has wandered long,
And from her God has gone!
But now with willing feet returns,
And now with deepest sorrow mourns
The deeds that she has done.

And will the Lord in pity look,
And blot her crimes out from His book,
And words of comfort say?
Ah yes; even now He pardon gives,
Even now the weeping sinner lives,
And wipes her tears away.

---

[2] See the parable of the Pharisee and publican. Luke 18.

And would the Lord thus deal with me,
If I should humbly bow my knee,
And all my sins confess?
For though I'm young I've wandered far,
My sins, I know, most hateful are
Unto God's holiness.

But if the Lord one mourner heard,
And sweetly spake the pardoning word,
Why should He not hear me?
He once was kind; (I well know this),
And what He was, He always is,
And evermore will be.

Questions

- How did the rich man behave to Jesus, after he asked Him to dine with him?
- What did the wicked woman do to Jesus?
- Why did she love Jesus so very much?
- Why did Jesus forgive her all her sin?
- Can Jesus forgive your sin?

God is merciful

A verse from the Bible for you to learn

Thou, Lord, art good, and ready to forgive; and plenteous in mercy unto all them that call upon Thee. Ps. 86:5.

Lesson 23

The Storm at Sea

Luke 8:22-25

Jesus often went into a ship with His disciples. Peter had a ship of his own, and John had another ship, and they liked to lend their ships to Jesus.

Once they were all in a ship, when the wind blew very hard and the water moved up and down, and came over the ship. The disciples were afraid that they would be drowned. Jesus had fallen asleep, and was lying on a pillow. The noise of the wind and of the water had not wakened Him.

His disciples went to Him and cried, 'O Master, dost Thou not care for us?' The disciples were afraid He would let them drown.

Then Jesus got up and said to the wind, 'Wind, be still!' And He said to the water, 'Be still!'

The wind stopped blowing, and the water was smooth and quiet. Then Jesus said to His disciples, 'Why were you afraid? Why did you not believe that I would take care of you?'

Jesus knew that they were tossed about, and He would have kept them safe though He was asleep.

The disciples said one to another, 'Jesus is the Son of God. Even the wind and the sea obey Him.'

The disciples, with Jesus their Lord,
At sea in a vessel were tossed;
The winds loudly blew, the waves too did roar;
They feared that they all should be lost.

The waters rushed into the ship;
For Jesus all eagerly look:
He lies on a pillow asleep.
Had He His disciples forsook?

He rises His work to perform:
The wind and the waters obey:
Soon hushed is the terrible storm,
The hurricane passes away.

How ready is Jesus to save!
How strong is His arm to protect!
His mercy we ever will crave;
And deliverance ever expect.

Questions

- What made the disciples afraid when they were in a ship?
- Was it wrong of them to be afraid?
- What did Jesus say to the wind and to the water?
- What did the disciples say when they saw the wind and the water obey Jesus?

What the disciples said of Jesus after the storm

A verse from the Bible for you to learn

He commandeth even the winds and water, and they obey Him. Luke 8:25.

LESSON 24

Jairus' Daughter

LUKE 8:41-56

A RICH man came to Jesus, and fell down at his feet and said, 'I have one little girl, and she is very sick; pray come and make her well.'

Jesus went with the rich man. When they were near the house, some servants came out and said, 'The little girl has just died; no one can make her well now.'

But Jesus said, 'Do not be afraid; I can make her well.'

He said to the father and mother of the little girl, 'Come with Me into the house. Peter, James, and John, you may come in, but no one else.'

So they went up into the room where the little girl was lying in bed. There were many people in the room playing sad music, singing sad songs, and crying, because the child was dead. But Jesus said, 'Stop crying. The girl is only sleeping; she is not dead.' Jesus said she was asleep, because He meant to make her alive again so soon. But the people laughed at Jesus. They said, 'She is dead.' They would not believe that He could make her alive again.

Jesus said, 'These people must be put out of the room.' So He sent them out and shut the door; but He let the father and mother, and Peter and James and John, stay in the room.

He took the little girl's hand and said, 'Arise!' First she sat up, and then she got out of bed and walked about the room. She was twelve years old. Jesus then said, 'Bring her something to eat.' The father and mother were very surprised at what had happened.

Hark! It is a father crying,
And this is what he says:
'My little daughter's lying
Just at the point of death.'

The Saviour soon consented
To come and heal the maid;
Nor was He ev'n prevented
By hearing she was dead.

He found the people weeping
Because her breath was gone,
And when He said, 'She's sleeping,'
They laughed him all to scorn.

The Lord no sinful mocker
Would suffer to remain;
Then by the hand He took her,
And made her rise again.

Ah, see the maid arising
According to His word!
Does not the deed surprising
Show Jesus to be Lord?

See, in their fond embraces
The parents clasp the maid:
Ashamed are now the faces
That mocked at what He said.

Questions

- Did Jesus ever make a dead child alive again?
- Who were sitting round her bed when Jesus came?
- Why did Jesus say that the girl was asleep?
- What did Jesus do to the people who laughed at Him?
- Who did Jesus allow to stay in the room?
- How old was the girl?

God does everything

A verse from the Bible for you to learn

The Lord killeth, and maketh alive: He bringeth down to the grave, and bringeth up. 1 Sam. 2:6.

LESSON 25

The Loaves and Fishes

MATTHEW 14:13-22

ONCE Jesus went into the wilderness with His disciples, and many people came after Him. Then Jesus preached to the people, and told them about His Father, and how He Himself had come down from heaven to save people from Satan. They listened to Him from morning till night.

When it was getting late, the disciples came to Jesus. They asked Him if He was going to send the people home. But Jesus knew that the people had nothing to eat all day, and He did not like to send them home tired and hungry. So He said to His disciples, 'Can you not feed them?'

'No,' they said, 'we have only five loaves and two small fishes, and see how many people there are!'

But Jesus said, 'Make them sit down on the grass, and bring the loaves and fishes to Me.' So the disciples made them all sit down.

There was a huge crowd of people. There were five thousand men, besides women and little children. How tired the little children must have been! It was time for them to have their supper and go to bed.

We shall hear how Jesus fed all these people.

They sat down on the green grass. Jesus took the loaves and fishes. First He lifted up His eyes to His Father, and thanked Him for the food.

He took a piece of bread and gave it to Peter. He said, 'Feed all those people sitting there'. He gave another piece to John and said, 'Feed those people'. He gave a piece of bread and fish to each of the disciples and told each to feed some people.

One little piece of bread would not be enough for all the children in this room. But Jesus made the bread to be enough for all the people. Every one had enough, and they threw on the grass a great many little pieces. But Jesus said to His disciples, 'Take some baskets and pick up the crumbs'. And they filled twelve baskets full of little bits of bread. Then Jesus told the people to go home.

How wonderful was the work Jesus had done! Yet you know that He feeds you, my little children, and all the people in the world.

How does He feed you?

He gives you bread.

What is bread made from?

From flour.

What is flour made from?

From wheat.

Who makes wheat?

God makes it grow in the fields.

Jesus is God; He makes the wheat grow;[1] so you see that Jesus feeds you. If He did not make wheat and the other food grow in the fields we would die.

But He will not forget us. He even remembers the little birds. They are not clever enough to plough, or to sow corn, or to reap, or to put corn into barns, yet God does not let them starve.[2] The birds cry to God, and He hears them, and lets them find food.[3] Now God loves us much better than He loves the little birds, because we have souls. So He will certainly hear us when we pray to Him.

If your mother had no bread in her house, and if she could not get money to buy some, yet God would hear her if she loved Him. He would not let her starve.[4] Will you not ask God for bread every day, and say. 'Give me this day my daily bread?'

---

[1] 'By Him all things consist.' Col. 1:17.

[2] 'Behold the fowls of the air: for they sow not, neither do they reap . . . yet your heavenly Father feedeth them. Are ye not much better than they?' Matt. 6:26.

[3] 'Who provideth for the raven his food? when his young ones cry unto God . . . .' Job 38:41.

[4] 'The righteous cry, and the Lord heareth.' Ps. 34:17. 'Which giveth food to the hungry.' Ps. 146:7.

We ought to thank God for the food we eat. Before we eat breakfast, or dinner, or supper, we should say, 'I thank Thee, O Lord, for this nice food.'

In listening they had spent the day;
Their homes far distant lie;
They would have fainted by the way
Without this kind supply.

Jesus, whose words they came to hear,
Has pity on their need;
He loves the weary heart to cheer,
The hungry poor to feed.

He gives them of His little store
By His disciples' hands.
Though little, He can make it more,
For all things He commands.

The Lord provides the beasts with food,
To Him the ravens cry;
He watches over us for good
And does our need supply.

Lord, save me from a selfish heart,
That nothing good can spare
To others may I give a part,
And all my comforts share.

Questions

- Did many people come to hear Jesus preach?
- Why did Jesus not like to send them home at night?
- How many loaves and fish did Jesus feed them with?
- Who gave the people the bread and fish?
- Did the people leave any of the bread?

- Where were the little pieces of bread put?
- What does God make grow in the fields?
- Could your mother give you bread if God did not make the corn grow?
- Does God feed any other creatures besides men, women, and children?
- Why does God take more care of you than of the birds?

How God feeds people and animals

A verse from the Bible for you to learn

He causeth the grass to grow for the cattle, and herb for the service of man: that He may bring forth food out of the earth. Ps. 104:14.

LESSON 26

The Kindness of Jesus

MATTHEW 15:21-28. MARK 10:13-16.

I TOLD you that the disciples were sometimes unkind, but Jesus was always kind.

Once a poor woman came crying after Jesus, saying, 'O Lord, I have a daughter who is very sick.' Jesus did not answer her at first. The disciples were unkind. They wished Jesus to send her away. She cried so loud that they said to Jesus, 'Send her away.'

The woman fell down at Jesus' feet, and said. 'Lord, help me!' And Jesus had pity on the woman. He said, 'I will do what you wish.'

The woman was glad to hear this, and she went home and found that her daughter was no longer sick.

Another time the disciples were unkind to some little children. Some poor women brought the children to Jesus, but the disciples were standing around, and they would not let the women come near. 'Go away,' they said; 'you must not bring the babies here to trouble us.'

But Jesus heard them speak, and He was very angry with the disciples. Jesus would not let the children go away. He said to the disciples, 'Suffer little children to come unto Me; do not send them away.'

Then He took the children in His arms, and put His hands on them, and prayed to His Father, and blessed them. O happy little children, to be taken into Jesus' arms!

Jesus loves children, and when the Holy Spirit makes them good and meek and gentle, they are Jesus' lambs. Jesus is their Shepherd, and He will take them to heaven when they die. [1]

Young children once to Jesus came,
His blessing to entreat;
And I may humbly do the same,
Before His mercy-seat.

For when their feeble hands were spread,
And bent each humble knee,
'Forbid them not,' the Saviour said;
And so He says to me.

Then, while His favour to implore,
My little hands are spread,
Do Thou Thy sacred blessing pour,
Dear Jesus, on my head.

---

[1] 'Ye my flock, the flock of my pasture, are men, and I am your God.' Ezek. 34:31. 'He shall feed His flock like a shepherd: He shall gather the lambs with His arm, and carry them in His bosom.' Isa. 40:11.

Questions

- Were the disciples as kind as Jesus?
- How did they behave to a woman who wanted Jesus to help her?
- What did they say to the women who brought their children to Jesus?
- What did Jesus say to the disciples when they were sending the children away?
- What did Jesus do to the children when they came to Him?
- Are there any children in heaven?

What Jesus said to His disciples when He called the children to Him

A verse from the Bible for you to learn

But Jesus called them unto Him, and said, Suffer little children to come unto Me, and forbid them not: for of such is the kingdom of God. Luke 18:16.

LESSON 27

The Lord's Prayer

MATTHEW 6:9-13, LUKE 11:1-13

WHEN Jesus was in the world, He loved to think of His Father in heaven. He liked to be alone, so that He might pray to His Father. Sometimes the tears ran down His cheeks while He prayed.[1]

[1] 'Who in the days of His flesh, when He had offered up prayers and supplications with strong crying and tears.' Heb 5:7.

One night Jesus prayed all night alone on the top of a high hill.[2] Sometimes Jesus prayed to His Father while His disciples stood near and listened.

Once when Jesus had been praying with them they said, 'Lord, teach us to pray.' Then Jesus taught them a little prayer. It was this: 'Our Father which art in heaven, hallowed be Thy name. Thy kingdom come. Thy will be done in earth, as it is in heaven. Give us this day our daily bread. And forgive us our debts, as we forgive our debtors. And lead us not into temptation, but deliver us from evil: for Thine is the kingdom, and the power, and the glory, for ever. Amen.'

I know that many little children say this prayer night and morning. Perhaps your mothers have taught you to say it. But did you know who said it first? It was Jesus, the Lord. So it is called 'the Lord's prayer.'

It is a very beautiful prayer, for Jesus said it; but it is hard for children to understand it. What is the meaning of 'Hallowed be Thy name'?

Let God's name be praised.

What are 'debts'?

Debts are what we owe to God because we have sinned.

Ask God to forgive your sins, or your debts.

Do you ever pray to God when you are alone?

You may pray to Him in any place — in the house or in the garden or anywhere else.

You may pray to Him at any time — in the night or in the middle of the day.

You may ask Him for anything you want, just as you ask your father or mother.[3]

What will you ask Him for? Will you ask Him to give you food and clothes and a house to live in?

---

[2] 'He went out into a mountain to pray, and continued all night in prayer to God.' Luke 6:12.

[3] 'How much more shall your heavenly Father give the Holy Spirit to them that ask Him?' Luke 11:13.

Yes, ask Him for all these things, but most of all ask Him for His Holy Spirit.

It is better to have the Holy Spirit than to have all the toys, all the money, all the flowers, all the birds, and all the beautiful things in the world.

Why is it better?

Because the Holy Spirit will make you love God, as the angels do, and will make you live for ever and ever.

Will you say this little prayer to God? 'O Lord, give me Thy Holy Spirit, for Christ's sake.'

Questions

- Why did Jesus choose to be alone sometimes?
- Did Jesus ever pray to His Father when His disciples were with Him?
- What did they ask Jesus to teach them?
- What prayer did Jesus teach them?
- What is the meaning of 'Hallowed be Thy name'?
- What must you ask God for, to make you good?
- Will God give you the Spirit if you ask Him?

When we should pray

A verse from the Bible for you to learn

Evening, and morning, and at noon, will I pray, and cry aloud: and He shall hear my voice. Ps. 55:17.

LESSON 28

Jesus Foretells His Death

MATTHEW 16:21-28.

JESUS knew everything that would happen,[1] and He knew that He must soon die. He used to tell His secrets to His disciples. So He took them to a place by themselves and said, 'I shall soon leave you. Wicked people will take Me and bind Me with ropes and beat Me and laugh at Me and nail Me to a cross, but I shall soon be alive again.'

The disciples could not bear to hear Jesus talk of dying, for they loved Him very much. They all looked very sad, and Peter said, 'Thou shalt not die'. But Jesus said, 'I must die to save sinners, and to please My Father.' The Father had desired Jesus to die, and He would not disobey His Father.[2]

Most of the people who wished to kill Jesus, lived in a city called Jerusalem. Jesus used to go to Jerusalem very often, and He used to preach there.

Why did some people hate Jesus?

Because He told them of their wickedness.[3] He used to say to them, 'You do not love God, who is My Father, but you are proud and vain.[4] You wish to kill Me. You tell lies. You are unkind to poor people. You pretend to love God, but while you are saying your prayers, you are thinking how good you

---

[1] 'Jesus therefore, knowing all things that should come upon Him.' John 18:4.

[2] 'I have power to lay it (my life) down, and I have power to take it again. This commandment have I received of My Father.' John 10:18.

[3] 'The world cannot hate you; but Me it hateth, because I testify of it, that the works thereof are evil.' John 7:7.

[4] 'I know you, that ye have not the love of God in you. . . . How can ye believe, which receive honour one of another?' John 5:42, 44.

are. Your hearts are full of wickedness. You are the children of the devil.'[5]

Jesus wished them to turn from their wickedness. He was sorry to see that they hated His Father, and that they would not turn from their wicked ways.[6]

The wicked people were angry with Jesus. They said that God was not His Father.[7] But Jesus said, 'He is My Father, and I came down from heaven, where He lives,[8] and I shall go back to Him some day.'[9]

At last the people took up stones to throw at Him, but Jesus did not choose to die yet, so He easily got away and went to a place where they could not find Him. He stayed there with His disciples for some time.[10]

Questions

- Did Jesus know that the wicked people would soon kill Him?
- Who did Jesus tell that He would die?
- Were they sorry?
- Why did many people hate Jesus?
- Who is the father of liars?

---

[5] 'Which devour widows' houses, and for a show make long prayers.' Luke 20:47. 'Their heart is far from Me.' Matt. 15:8. 'Even so ye also outwardly appear righteous unto men, but within ye are full of hypocrisy and iniquity.' Matt. 23:28. 'But now ye seek to kill Me. . . . Ye are of your father the devil, and the lusts of your father ye will do. He was a murderer from the beginning . . . he is a liar.' John 8:40, 44.

[6] 'Being grieved for the hardness of their hearts.' Mark 3:3. 'And ye will not come to Me, that ye might have life. John 5:40.

[7] 'The Jews sought the more to kill Him, because He . . . said also that God was His Father.' John 5:18.

[8] 'I proceeded forth and came from God.' 'I am from above.' John 8:42, 23.

[9] 'What and if ye shall see the Son of man ascend up where He was before?' John 6:62.

[10] 'Then the Jews took up stones again to stone Him. . . . He escaped out of their hand, and went away again beyond Jordan.' John 10:31, 39, 40.

- How did the wicked people try to kill Jesus?
- Did Jesus let them kill Him?
- Why did He hide in a place far away?

Where Jesus came from, and where He went

A verse from the Bible for you to learn

I came forth from the Father, and am come into the world: again, I leave the world, and go to the Father. John 16:28.

LESSON 29

Lazarus

JOHN 11:1-17

JESUS stayed with His disciples in a place by Himself. The wicked people who wanted to kill Him could not find Him, but Jesus' friends knew where He was.

Jesus had others friends besides His disciples. One of His friends was called Lazarus. Lazarus had two sisters; their names were Martha and Mary. These three all lived together. They all loved Jesus, and Jesus loved them. Jesus used often to come to see them. He used to sit in their house and talk to them. Martha liked to make a fine dinner when Jesus came, but Mary liked to sit and listen to His sweet words. [1]

---

[1] Luke 10:38-42.

One day Lazarus fell very sick. Martha and Mary loved their brother Lazarus very much indeed. They knew that Jesus could make Lazarus well; so they sent a man to tell Jesus that Lazarus was sick. The man went far away to look for Jesus.

Lazarus grew worse and worse. At last he died. His friends wrapped white cloths round his face and his arms and his legs. They put him in a big hole and rolled a stone up to it to close the hole.

Martha and Mary waited and longed for Jesus to come. Four days passed, and at last Jesus came. Martha and Mary did not think that Jesus would now make Lazarus alive again, because their brother had been dead for so long. So they sat on the ground and cried.

When Martha heard that Jesus was on the road a little way off, she came to Jesus and said. 'If Thou hadst been here, my brother had not died.' She knew that even then God would do anything that Jesus asked Him.

Then Jesus said, 'Your brother shall rise again.'

'Yes,' said Martha, 'I know he will rise again at the last day, when all the dead people will rise.' Martha was afraid that Jesus would not choose to make Lazarus alive soon, but she knew that He was able to do it.

Martha went back to the house and found Mary still sitting on the ground, and many friends around her. Martha whispered in her ear, and told her that Jesus wanted to speak to her. So Martha and Mary went together and found Jesus waiting for them on the road.

Mary's friends went with her, and they cried, and Mary cried very much indeed. When she saw Jesus she fell down at His feet and said, 'Lord, if Thou hadst been here my brother had not died.'

Jesus was very sorry to see her so unhappy and to see so many people crying. He felt very sad indeed, and He sighed very deeply. Jesus does not like to see any one in trouble; He is so kind.

Then Jesus said, 'Where have you put Lazarus?'

Martha and Mary and their friends said, 'Come and see.' Then they showed Him the way to the grave. As Jesus walked along, the tears rolled down His cheeks.

At last they came to the grave. It was a hole, and a very large stone was in front of the hole. Then Jesus said, 'Take away the stone.'

Martha thought that Jesus was going to look at Lazarus lying dead. So she said, 'Do not go in; his flesh has a bad smell by this time. He has been dead for four days.' But Jesus told her to believe that He could make Lazarus alive.

They then rolled away the stone. Jesus lifted up His eyes to His Father in heaven, and thanked Him for helping Him to do wonderful things.

Many people were standing by, looking at Jesus, and wondering what He would do. Poor Martha and Mary were longing to see Lazarus alive again. Then Jesus spoke loudly and said, 'Lazarus, come forth.'

Lazarus heard, though he was dead; for the dead hear the voice of Jesus. Lazarus got up and walked to the opening of the hole. His hands were tied with cloths, and his feet wrapped round with cloths, and a cloth was over his face. But Jesus said, 'Undo the cloths.'

How pleased Martha and Mary must have been to see his face again! How they must have thanked the Lord Jesus for His kindness!

The people who saw all this were surprised, and they said, 'Jesus must be the Son of God.'

Questions

- Had Lazarus any sisters?
- What were their names?
- Did Jesus ever come to their house?
- When Lazarus was sick, was Jesus with him, or far away?
- Was Lazarus dead before Jesus came?
- Did Martha think that Jesus could make Lazarus alive again?

- Why did Jesus sigh and weep?
- Where was dead Lazarus put?
- What did Jesus say to Lazarus?
- What clothes did Lazarus wear in the grave?
- What did the people think of Jesus when they saw Him make Lazarus alive again?

God's care of the righteous

A verse from the Bible for you to learn

The righteous cry, and the Lord heareth, and delivereth them out of all their troubles. Ps. 34:17.

LESSON 30

Jesus Enters Jerusalem

MATTHEW 21:1-11, 14-17

WHICH was one of the greatest miracles that Jesus ever did?

It was making Lazarus alive again; because he had been dead for four days.

Many of the wicked people who hated Jesus heard of it, but then they hated Him more than ever. They said, 'We must kill Him soon, or every one will believe that He is the Son of God.' Jesus knew that they wanted to kill Him, so He went and hid Himself in a place they did not know about. They looked for Him, but they could not find Him.

But could Jesus always stay in that quiet place, where He was living with His disciples?

No, He came down to this world to die for sinners. He only waited till the time came for Him to die. Then He said to His disciples, 'We must go up to Jerusalem, and I shall be mocked and beaten and killed, but I shall come out of My grave after three days.'

The disciples did not like to hear this, but they chose to go with Jesus wherever He went. Jesus walked along the road and at last He came near Jerusalem. Then He stopped and said to His disciples, 'I shall ride into Jerusalem on an ass.' Jesus had no ass of His own; He always walked from place to place. But Jesus could put it into a man's heart to lend Him one.

He said to two of His disciples, 'Go along the road a little way, and you will see an ass and a young ass tied, and a man standing near. Bring the ass and the young one to Me, for I know that the man will let them come.'

So the two disciples went. When they had gone a little way they saw an ass tied up, and a young one with it. They began to untie the ass, but a man standing near them said, 'Why do you untie the ass?'

They said, 'The Lord has need of them.' Then the man let them go. I suppose that man loved the Lord Jesus and liked to lend Him his things.

The two disciples brought the asses to Jesus. They took off some of their clothes and put them on the young ass, and Jesus sat on it.

Many people came out of Jerusalem to see Jesus, for they heard that He had made Lazarus alive again. The people began to praise Jesus and to call Him King. They took off some of their clothes and laid them down on the road for the ass to walk on. And they pulled branches off the trees that grew near and laid them on the road too.

So Jesus came to the great town of Jerusalem. All the people came into the streets to look at Him. Even the little children began to praise Him, and to call Him King.

The proud men that hated Jesus were very angry at hearing all these praises. They did not like to hear Jesus praised. They came to Him and said, 'Why dost Thou let these children call Thee King?'

But Jesus liked to hear the children sing His praise. So He would not tell them to be silent. Jesus loved little children, and these little children loved Jesus.

Questions

- What did some of the people in Jerusalem wish to do to Jesus?
- Did Jesus walk or ride into Jerusalem?
- Where did the disciples find an ass?
- Why did so many of the people come to see Jesus when He was riding on the ass?
- What did the people lay upon the road?
- How did the little children make the proud men angry?

The people who should praise God

A verse from the Bible for you to learn

Both young men, and maidens; old men, and children: let them praise the name of the Lord. Ps. 148:12,13.

LESSON 31

The Temple

LUKE 19:47, 48; 20:19, 20; 21:37, 38

THERE was a large place in Jerusalem, like a large church, called the Temple. It was white outside, and very beautiful. The doors were open all day, and people used to go there to pray to God. It was God's house. Jesus used often to be there with His disciples. Poor, blind, and lame people came to Him there. Jesus cured them all, and talked to them about His Father.

The little children sang His praises in the Temple. All day long Jesus taught the people about God, and they listened to what He said. They liked to hear Him.

The wicked and proud men came to the Temple to laugh at Jesus. They spoke rudely to Him, but He bore it all as meekly as a lamb.

At night He left the Temple and went out of the town to a high hill, where He prayed to God alone in the dark.

The wicked men longed to catch Jesus to kill Him. They said to each other, 'How can we get Him? The people will not let us take hold of Him if they see us, or we would go to the temple to catch Him. If we could find Him alone in the dark, then we would put ropes on Him and take Him to the judge.' This is what the wicked people said to each other as they sat together.

Questions

- Where was the Temple?
- What did people do in it?
- Did Jesus go there often?
- Who came there to laugh at Jesus?
- Where did Jesus go at night?
- Why did the wicked men not take Jesus when He was in the Temple?
- Did the wicked men know where Jesus went at night?

Wicked people are cruel

A verse from the Bible for you to learn

The wicked watcheth the righteous, and seeketh to slay him.
Ps. 37:32.

LESSON 32

Judas

JOHN 12:6, MATTHEW 26:3, 4, 14-16

JESUS had twelve disciples. Did they all love Him?

Peter loved Jesus, and John loved Him, and all the rest loved Him[1] except one. His name was Judas. He did not love Jesus, but only pretended to love Him. He was like the devil.[2]

Did Jesus know how wicked Judas was?

Yes, He saw into his heart. But the disciples thought Judas was good,[3] for Judas used to kiss the Lord Jesus. He used to speak kindly to Him and talk about God like the rest.

But Judas loved something; he loved money. He wanted to get a lot of money. He was covetous, and he was a thief. The disciples had a bag, and when they had money they put it in the bag. All the disciples put their money in the same bag. But there was very little money in the bag, for they were very poor. Judas used to take care of the bag. He used to steal some of the money out of it and keep it for himself. But no one found him out or thought he was a thief, except Jesus, and He knew it well.

Judas was always thinking, 'How shall I get money?' One day, when the proud men were sitting together, Judas came in. Judas said to them, 'You want to find Jesus when He is alone. Will you give me some money, and I will show you where He goes at night?'

The proud people said, 'Yes, we will.'

Judas said, 'How much money will you give me?'

They said, 'Thirty pieces of silver.'

---

[1] 'The Father Himself loveth you, because ye have loved Me.' John 16:27.

[2] 'Have not I chosen you twelve, and one of you is a devil?' John 6:70.

[3] This is evident, from the disciples trusting Judas with the bag, and from their failing to suspect him of treachery to their Lord, when one of their number was accused.

Then Judas said, 'Some night I will bring you to Jesus when He is alone.'

The wicked people were very glad to hear this.

'Now,' they thought, 'we shall soon catch Him and kill Him.'

Judas went back to Jesus, but he did not tell the disciples what he had done. But Jesus knew what he had done. Jesus could see all his thoughts. He knew all that Judas did, both by day and by night. Yet Jesus did not tell Judas that He knew his wicked plans.

When Jesus on the earth abode,
Some friends He had, though few;
Their love, alas, too faintly flowed,
Yet was sincere and true.

But there was one whose heart was cold,
Who did not love his Lord,
But sought of silver and of gold
To make a plenteous hoard.

His wicked thoughts he hid from all,
And piously would speak;
The Saviour 'Lord and Master' call,
And even kiss His cheek.

In vain he thus his love declared,
And fond attention paid;
In vain in toil and danger shared,
In vain he preached and prayed.

Full well the blessed Saviour knew
He was by sin enchained,
And from the bag in secret drew
The money it contained.

He saw him in the depth of night,
To gain a base reward,
Promise the Jews to please their spite,
And to betray his Lord.

Thus Judas gold and silver chose,
Instead of joys above,
And plunged his soul in endless woes,
And lost his Master's love.

And such will be my wretched end
(Whatever I appear),
If God I care not to offend,
And man alone I fear.

If I, like Judas, talk and pray,
And yet in secret steal,
I shall be punished in that day
When God shall all reveal.

Questions

- Did all Jesus' disciples love Him?
- Did the other disciples know that Judas did not love Jesus?
- Did Jesus know it?
- Was Judas a thief?
- What did Judas love better than anything else?
- What did Judas promise He would do for the wicked people if they would give him money?
- How much money did they promise to give Him?
- Did Jesus know that Judas meant to show the wicked people where He was at night?

God can see all things

A verse from the Bible for you to learn

The darkness hideth not from Thee: but the night shineth as the day. Ps. 139:12.

LESSON 33

The Last Supper

PART 1 — LUKE 22:7-14. JOHN 13:1-17

JESUS said to His disciples, 'I am soon going to be killed, but before I die I shall eat a supper with you in Jerusalem.'

Then Jesus said to Peter and John, 'Go and get the supper ready'. But they said, 'Where shall we get it ready?' Jesus had no house in Jerusalem, but He knew how to find a room.

So Jesus said to Peter and John, 'Go into Jerusalem, and you will meet a man carrying a jug. Go after him; he will go into a house. The master of the house will lend Me a room. Tell him that I am going to die, and that I want to eat a supper with My disciples.'

Then Peter and John went into Jerusalem. Who did they meet?

A man carrying a jug.

They followed him. He went into a house. Peter and John went in after him, and they said to him, 'Jesus wants a room to eat a supper in with His disciples, before His death.'

Then the master took them upstairs, and showed them a large room. There was a table in it and seats all round the table. There was a jug, and a basin to wash their feet in, and a cup and dishes.

Peter and John got some bread and wine and other things, and made the supper ready. Then they went back and told Jesus (who was in the country, not far away) that supper was ready. So Jesus and all His disciples came to the house in the evening. They went upstairs, and they all sat down. Jesus loved John better than all the rest, and John sat next to Jesus.

After they had been a little while at supper, Jesus got up and took a towel and tied it round His waist. He took a jug and poured water into a basin, and He began to wash His disciples' feet, and to wipe them with the towel round His waist. But when He came to Peter, Peter said, 'Thou shalt never wash my feet.'

Peter thought it was too kind of Jesus to wash his feet, as if He was a servant. Jesus was not proud, but He loved to be kind to His disciples. Then Jesus said to Peter, 'If I wash you not, you cannot be Mine. But I have made you clean already.' Jesus had made Peter's heart clean. Now Peter was glad that Jesus should wash his feet.

All the disciples had clean hearts, except Judas. His heart was full of wickedness; Satan was in it. Yet Jesus washed Judas' feet. He was kind even to wicked Judas, who hated Him.

When Jesus had washed all the disciples' feet, He sat down again and began to talk to them. He said, 'Do you know what I have done to you? I have washed your feet, though I am your Lord and Master. I wish to teach you to be as kind to each other as I have been to you.'

When the sad hour was almost come
That Jesus must depart,
He gathered in an upper room
Those dearest to His heart.

Ah, great was their astonishment,
When, rising from His seat,
Upon the floor He lowly bent
To wash His servants' feet.

Beside the board again He sat,
And thus expressed His mind:
'If I, your Lord, upon you wait,
O, should not you be kind?

'O, let the love that I have shown
By you remembered be;
And by your love let it be known
That you belong to Me.'

Questions

- Did Jesus have a house in Jerusalem?
- How did He get a room to eat a supper in with His disciples before He died?
- Who did He send to find the room?
- How did Peter and John find out which house they were to go to?
- What things were in the room?
- Who sat next to Jesus at supper?
- How many people were at the supper?
- Why did Jesus pour water into a basin?
- Why did Peter not like Jesus to wash his feet?
- Had Jesus made His disciples' hearts clean?
- Was Judas' heart clean?
- Why did Jesus wash His disciples' feet?
- What commandment did Jesus give to His disciples?

Christ's last command

A verse from the Bible for you to learn

This is My commandment, That ye love one another, as I have loved you. John 15:12.

Lesson 34

The Last Supper

Part 2 — John 13:21-30

YOU know the wicked thing that Judas meant to do. Jesus knew that he would bring the wicked people to take Him and kill Him. Jesus had been very kind to Judas, and Jesus was sorry that he was so wicked.

Jesus was sitting at supper, and all the twelve disciples were round the table. He said, 'One of you will give Me to the wicked men to be killed! One of you, My disciples.'

All the disciples were very sorry, and Peter said, 'Is it I?' And John said, 'Is it I?' And each of them said, 'Is it I?' But Jesus did not tell them.

Now John was leaning his head on Jesus' bosom, and Peter whispered to John, 'Do ask the Lord which it is that will show the wicked people where He is.'

So John whispered, 'Which is it?'

Then Jesus said, 'The one that dips some bread in the dish with Me.' For there was a dish of sauce on the table, and Jesus dipped His bread in it. As He dipped it, one of the disciples put his hand in the dish too. Which was it?

It was Judas; he dipped his bread in the dish with Jesus. So John knew which of the disciples was so wicked.

Then Jesus said to Judas, 'Go, and do what you mean to do.' Judas got up and went out of the room.

Where did he go?

He went to the wicked people, to bring them to Jesus in the dark. But the disciples thought he was going to buy something at a shop, or to give money to the poor.

Questions

- At supper what did Jesus say that one of His disciples would do?

- Who asked Jesus to tell him which it was?
- Who dipped his hand in the dish with Jesus?
- Why did Judas go out of the room?
- What did the disciples think he was going to do?

Only God knows us completely

A verse from the Bible for you to learn

Thou, even Thou only, knowest the hearts of all the children of men. 1 Kings 8:39.

LESSON 35

The Last Supper

PART 3 — MATTHEW 26:26-36. JOHN 14:14; 18:1-3

AFTER supper Jesus took some bread and broke it in little bits. He gave a piece to each of the disciples and said, 'This is My body. I am going to die; eat this, and think of Me.'

Then Jesus poured some wine into a cup and told them all to drink out of it. He said, 'This is My blood; I shall soon bleed and die. Drink this, and think of Me.'

Jesus said, 'I shall not eat a supper with you again before I die. I am going to My Father. I must leave you, but I shall come back again.' Then they all sang together.

Afterwards Jesus got up from the table and went downstairs into the street, and the disciples followed Him. It was dark, but Jesus talked to them as they went along. He said, 'I am going to die tonight, and you will all leave Me.'

But Peter said, 'I will not leave Thee. I will go to prison with Thee. I will die with Thee, but I will never leave Thee.'

Jesus said to him, 'Yes, you will, Peter. You will say that you do not know Me. You will say that you are not My friend. This night, Peter, you will say so before the cock crows.' (Cocks crow in the morning, when daylight comes.)

Jesus talked kindly to His disciples. He said, 'Do not be sorry because I am going away. I shall go back to My Father, and I shall soon come back to you. When I am in heaven, I shall get ready a place in heaven for you. I command you to love one another, and I will send the Holy Spirit to comfort you.'

At last Jesus came to a garden. He had often been to that garden with His disciples, and wicked Judas knew the place. Where was Judas now?

He was with the proud, wicked men.

You will soon hear how he came to the garden, and how he brought the servants of the wicked men with him. Those wicked men meant to send their servants to catch Jesus.

'This is My flesh,' the sorrowing Saviour said,
And as He spoke, He gave the broken bread.
'This is My blood,' and then He made all drink,
And of their dying Master ever think.

'This night I die; this night My body's bruised;
This night by wicked men My name's abused;
And even you, My dearest friends, shall fly,
And leave your Master all alone to die.'

His friends in sorrow heard; then promised
With Him they fondly loved their blood to shed;
And Peter loudest said, 'With Thee I'll die,'
And little thought he should his Lord deny.

Questions

- What did Jesus break into pieces and give to His disciples?
- What did He give them to drink?
- What was the bread like?

- What was the wine like?
- Where did Jesus go after supper?
- What did He tell His disciples as He walked along the road?
- What did Peter say he would do, if Jesus was killed or taken prisoner?
- What did Jesus tell Peter that he would say?
- Where would Jesus go after He was killed?
- Would Jesus forget His disciples when He was in heaven?
- What did Jesus say He would send into their hearts?
- Where did Jesus take His disciples?

What Jesus said He would do for His disciples in heaven

A verse from the Bible for you to learn

I go to prepare a place for you. John 14:2.

LESSON 36

The Garden

MATTHEW 26:30-57. JOHN 18:12

WHEN Jesus came to the garden, He told all His disciples to stay where they were till He came back. But He took three of them with Him.

Who were they?

Peter, James and John. He took them further on in the garden. Then He said to them, 'I feel very sad indeed. I am going to pray. Do you stay here. Do not go to sleep, but pray while I am praying.'

Then Jesus went a little way off by Himself, and fell upon the ground and began to pray to His Father to help Him. He ended His prayer by saying, 'O Father, not as I will, but as Thou wilt.'[1] He prayed very earnestly, and He felt so unhappy that the blood came out of His skin and fell onto the ground. Then He got up and went back to Peter and James and John, but He found them asleep. He woke them and told them to pray.

Then He went back and prayed again to His Father. He asked His Father to help Him in His great sorrow. When He came back to His disciples, they had fallen asleep again.

Then Jesus prayed again, and His Father sent an angel from heaven to comfort Him. I do not know what the angel said, but I know the angel loved Him. The angel could speak sweet words to Him and tell Him how His Father loved Him. The angel did not stay long; he soon went back to God.

Then Jesus came again to His disciples and found them asleep again. But Jesus woke them and told them to get up. 'Judas,' He said, 'is near.'

While Jesus was saying this, many people came walking into the garden. These were the servants of the wicked men in Jerusalem. They had swords and sticks and lights in their hands. And Judas went in front of them to show them where Jesus was. But Judas came up to Jesus in a very sly way. He gave Him a kiss, pretending to love Him.

Jesus knew what Judas was doing, and He said, 'Friend, why do you come here? And why do you kiss Me?'

Jesus did not run away, but He went up to the wicked men and said, 'Who are you looking for?'

They said, 'For Jesus.'

He said, 'I am He.'

When He said that, God made all the wicked people fall on the ground on their backs. Then Jesus could have run away. But He chose to stay, so that He might die for His people.

---

[1] 'Who in the days of His flesh, when he had offered up prayers and supplications with strong crying and tears unto Him that was able to save Him from death.' Heb. 5:7.

The wicked people soon got up. God let them get up; but Jesus said to them, 'If you want to have Me, you must let My disciples go away.'

It was kind of Jesus to think of them, and they were frightened and glad to get away. They did not wish to stay to die with Jesus.

But Peter took a sword and cut off one of the wicked men's ears. Peter wished to fight; but Jesus said, 'Put up your sword. If I were to pray now to My Father, He would send thousands of angels to help Me.'[2] Then Jesus touched the man's ear, and made it all right again.

Why did not Jesus pray to God to send the angels?

Because He chose to die to save people from their sins. If the angels had come and taken Jesus back to heaven, then we should all have gone to hell.

Peter and all the rest of the disciples ran away and left Jesus all alone with the wicked men. They took ropes and tied His hands and feet, and they led Him away into Jerusalem. Jesus went along as meekly as a lamb.

'What, could ye not watch with Me one hour?'
Matt. 26:40

Could they not watch one little hour
With Him they soon should see no more
Upon this earth beneath?
Not watch with Him in His distress,
Who was all love and tenderness,
And still did pity breathe?

But hear the Saviour gently speak;
He says, though willing they are weak,
And bids them rise and pray.

---

[2] 'The cup which My Father hath given Me, shall I not drink it?' John 18:11

Oh, now the hour of prayer is past,
The enemy is come at last
To take the Lord away.

Oh, how I love the patience rare,
With which I see the Saviour bear
His friends' unkind neglect!
Though He to them such love has shown,
He might when suffering thus alone
Their tenderest care expect.

And when my angry passions rise
I'll set the Lord before my eyes,
His gentle voice I'll hear;
And the same patience try to show,
If left alone in pain or woe
By my companions dear.

Questions

- How many disciples did Jesus take with Him to another part of the garden?
- What did Jesus tell them to do while He was praying?
- What did Jesus pray to His Father about?
- Did Peter and James and John pray while Jesus was praying?
- How many times did Jesus come back to Peter and James and John?
- Who came from heaven to comfort Him?
- Who came into the garden at last?
- Why did Judas kiss Jesus?
- Did Jesus know why Judas kissed Him?
- What did Jesus call Judas?
- Did Jesus run away from the wicked men?
- Who made the wicked people fall down on the ground?

- Did they get up again soon?
- Did the disciples run away?
- What did Peter cut off with his sword?
- Did Jesus wish Peter to fight for Him?
- What did Jesus do to the man's ear?
- Where did the wicked people take Jesus?
- What was Jesus like, when He went so meekly with them?

The meekness of Jesus when He died

A verse from the Bible for you to learn

He is brought as a lamb to the slaughter, and as a sheep before her shearers is dumb, so He openeth not His mouth.
Isa. 53:7.

LESSON 37

Peter's Denial

MATTHEW 26:57-75

THE wicked, proud men who hated Jesus sat up all night. They sent their servants with some soldiers to fetch Jesus. They were in a fine house, seated on seats round the room, talking together and longing for Jesus to be brought.

They said one to another, 'We will have Him killed when He comes. We will take Him to the judge.'

At last Jesus came in with the wicked servants. The proud men were glad to see Him. They made Him stand up in the middle of the large room. Then they spoke roughly to Him. 'Art Thou the Son of God?' they said.

'Yes,' said Jesus, 'I am; and one day you will see Me coming in the clouds with the angels.'

Then the wicked men were angry. 'Do you hear what He says?' they cried out. 'He calls Himself the Son of God. He must be taken to the judge to be killed.'

Jesus stood meekly all this time and hardly spoke a word. But what happened to the disciples?

They ran away.

Did Peter run away? Peter said he would die with Jesus. But he ran away too. At last Peter thought, 'I will go and look for Jesus. I should like to see what the wicked men are doing to Him.'

So Peter came to Jerusalem and into the fine house. He came into the hall first. The wicked servants were sitting round a fire in the hall. A door was open, and through the door Peter could see Jesus. There He was, standing before the wicked men. Peter hoped that nobody would know that he was one of Jesus' disciples. He was afraid that he too would be killed. But, as Peter was sitting by the fire warming himself, a maid said to him, 'You are one of Jesus' disciples.'

Peter was frightened and said, 'No, I am not. I do not know the man you speak of.'

Then Peter got up and went outside the door, but another maid said to him, 'I am sure you are one of the disciples of Jesus.'

'No,' said Peter, 'I am not.' So Peter went back again to the fire and began talking with the servants.

But some of them remembered having seen Peter in the garden, and they came to Peter and said, 'We are certain that you are one of the disciples.' And one of them said to him, 'I saw you in the garden.'

Then Peter began to swear, and to say that he was not one of the disciples. But while Peter was speaking so wickedly he heard a cock crow.

Peter remembered what Jesus had said, and he looked at Jesus. Then Jesus turned round His face and looked at Peter. It was such a look! Jesus did not speak, but His look seemed to say, 'Is this Peter, My friend, who said he would die with Me? Is this his love for Me? Is he saying that he does not know Me?'

Peter felt very sorry; he felt as if his heart would break. He went out of the house and began to cry very much indeed. Peter really did love Jesus; only Satan had tempted him to be so wicked as to say that he did not know Jesus.

If Peter had prayed in the garden instead of going to sleep, he would have behaved better. But Christ had often prayed for Peter, so that Satan might not get his soul at last. [1]

Questions

- Did the proud men go into the garden themselves, or did they send their servants?
- What had they been doing all night?
- When Jesus came to Jerusalem, where did He stand?
- Did they ask Him if He was the Son of God?
- Did He say that He was?
- What did the wicked men say must be done to Jesus?
- Where was Peter all this time?
- Could Peter see Jesus?
- Did Peter wish people to know that he was one of Jesus' disciples?
- Why not?
- Did any one ask Peter who he was?
- What did Peter say?
- How many times did people ask Peter who he was?
- What did Peter hear that made him feel how bad he had been?
- What did Peter do after Jesus looked at him?

---

[1] 'Satan hath desired to have you . . . but I have prayed for thee, that thy faith fail not.' Luke 22:31,32.

- Did Peter really love Jesus?
- Who had often prayed for Peter?
- Did Satan get Peter's soul at last?

How Peter repented of his sin

A verse from the Bible for you to learn

And the Lord turned, and looked upon Peter. And Peter went out, and wept bitterly. Luke 22:61, 62.

LESSON 38

Pontius Pilate

JOHN 18:22-40. MATTHEW 26:67, 68. JOHN 19:1-16

ALL night long, Jesus stood in the great room. He heard all Peter said, and that must have made Him sad. The wicked people were like lions and tigers, but Jesus was like a lamb. They looked at Him as if they hated Him.[1] Once when He spoke, a servant slapped His face, but Jesus bore this meekly.

The judge was not up yet, because it was night. So the wicked people were forced to wait till the morning. That night the servants came round Jesus and beat Him and pushed Him and laughed at Him. They even spat in His face.

When the morning came, the wicked people said, 'Now we will bring Him to the judge.'

---

[1] 'They gaped upon Me with their mouths, as a ravening and a roaring lion.' Ps. 22:13. 'They gnashed upon Me with their teeth.' Ps. 35:16.

So they went out of their fine house and took Jesus with them.

The judge sat upon a high seat in the street. His name was Pontius Pilate. The judge did not know Jesus. The judge said, 'What has He done?'

The wicked people said, 'He calls himself a king.'

Then Pilate said to Jesus, 'Art Thou a king?'

Jesus said, 'Yes, I am.' But Pilate was sure that Jesus had done nothing wrong, so he did not want to punish Him.

Then the wicked men made a great noise and said, 'You must crucify Him!'

'No,' said Pilate, 'I will beat Him, and that will be enough.' So Pilate gave Jesus to some soldiers. They took Him into a house and beat Him with knotted ropes (this way of beating is called scourging) and the blood ran all down His back. Then the cruel soldiers laughed at Him because He said He was a king. They took off His own clothes, and put some fine clothes on Him, such as kings wear, purple and red.

Then they said, 'We must put a crown on His head.' So they took prickly thorns, sharp like pins, and twisted them together to make a crown. They put it on His head.

They said, 'He must have a sceptre' (for kings hold in their hands a rod called a sceptre). So they put a reed in His hand for a sceptre. Then they took it from Him and beat Him on the head. And they knelt down to Him laughing; they said, 'O king! O king!'

Pilate saw the soldiers tormenting Jesus, and he brought Him into the street, where the wicked people were. He showed Jesus to them and said, 'Behold, look at your King!'

Pilate hoped they would be sorry for Him, because blood was on His forehead from the thorns, His back had been scourged, and He was dressed in fine clothes to mock Him. But the wicked people were cruel like tigers.

'No,' they said, 'crucify Him, crucify Him!' All the people cried out, 'Crucify Him!' though Jesus had always been so kind to them.

'Will you crucify your king?' asked Pilate.

'He is not our king!' the people said.

There was a very great noise in the street, from the people all speaking at once. Then Pilate thought he would please the wicked people, so he said, 'Take Him and crucify Him.' Then the people were glad. But first the soldiers took the fine clothes off Jesus and put His own clothes on Him again.

How wicked it was of Pilate to let Him be crucified! Pilate thought Jesus was good, yet he let Him be killed to please the people.

What! is there none to take His part
Who silent, trembling bleeding, stands?
Not one to cheer His broken heart,
Or snatch Him from those cruel hands?

A thousand voices lifted high
Now fill with horrid shouts the air:
'Away with Him and crucify!'
Nor does one friend for Him appear.

Behold how men His love reward!
His tender flesh the scourge has torn,
His gentle hands are bound with cord,
His head is crowned with prickly thorn.

And when I hear one, smiling, tell
Of sinful things that men have done,
I will not smile, but sorrow feel,
Because sin bruised God's only Son.

Questions

- Did Jesus stand a long time before the wicked people?
- How did one of the servants behave to Him?
- When did the wicked men take Him to the judge?
- What did the servants put over His face?
- Where was the judge sitting?

- What was the judge's name?
- Did the judge wish to hurt Jesus?
- What did the wicked people say that Jesus had called Himself?
- Was Jesus a king?
- What is scourging?
- Why did the soldiers laugh at Him?
- What clothes did they put on Him?
- What did they put on His head?
- What did they put in His hand?
- What is a sceptre?
- Why did Pilate tell the wicked people to look at Jesus?
- Did the people make a great noise?
- What did Pilate at last say should be done to Jesus?
- Why did Pilate allow Jesus to be crucified?

How Jesus was treated before He died

A verse from the Bible for you to learn

I hid not My face from shame and spitting. Isa. 50:6.

Lesson 39

Death of Judas

Matthew 27:3-5

WHERE was Judas all this time? The wicked people had given him the money, thirty pieces of silver. But Judas could not be happy.

'Ah!' thought he, 'I have killed my good Master! What a wicked thing I have done!'

Judas felt that he could not like the money. He could not bear to keep it, because he had done such a wicked thing to get it. So Judas went to look for the wicked men. They had been sitting up all night talking against Jesus, but now they were in God's house — the Temple.

Judas brought the thirty pieces of silver in his hands and threw them down on the floor near the wicked men. Judas said, 'I have done a very wicked thing.'

But the men did not care for that. All they wanted was to get Jesus killed. They picked up the pieces of silver from the floor. Then they went to buy a field with the money.

And where did Judas go?

He went out to the field to kill himself. He did not go and ask Jesus to forgive him, but he went and hanged himself.[1] O what a horrible sight it must have been! But it was more horrible to think where Judas' soul had gone.

It had gone to hell — to Satan.

It was very wicked of Judas to hang himself, instead of praying to God to forgive him.

Judas is in the wicked place now;[2] and Jesus will judge him at the last day and say, 'Depart, you cursed one!'

Questions

- Was Judas happy when he got the thirty pieces of silver?
- What did he do with them?
- How did Judas kill himself?
- Where is Judas now?

The misery of the wicked

A verse from the Bible for you to learn

There is no peace, saith my God, to the wicked. Isa. 57:21.

---

[1] 'And falling headlong, he burst asunder in the midst, and all his bowels gushed out.' Acts 1:18.

[2] 'This ministry and apostleship, from which Judas by transgression fell, that he might go to his own place.' Acts 1:25.

Lesson 40

The Cross

Part 1 — Luke 23:26-34

THE wicked people were very glad when Pilate said that Jesus was to be crucified. They made a cross of two great pieces of wood and made Jesus carry it. They took him out of Jerusalem into the country. The wicked people came with Him.

Jesus was so weak that He could hardly walk, and the cross was so heavy that He could not carry it. He would have dropped down on the way if a man had not helped Him to carry the cross.

There were a few people who were sorry for the Lord Jesus. Some women, who loved Him very much, came crying after Him. Jesus heard them crying, and He turned round and spoke very kindly to them.

He said, 'Do not cry for Me; cry for yourselves and for your children.' Why did Jesus tell them to cry for themselves?

Jesus knew how God would one day punish the people in Jerusalem for their wickedness.

At last Jesus came to the top of a hill. Then the soldiers made Jesus lie on His cross, and they put nails in His hands and nails in His feet. So they nailed Him to the cross. Then the soldiers made a hole in the ground and stuck the cross in it.

They had taken off Jesus' clothes. And when He was on the cross, four soldiers tore the clothes in four pieces. They each took a piece. But when they looked at His coat they said, 'We will not tear it, because there is no seam in it'. Then one of the soldiers took it for his own. So the wicked people took everything away from Jesus.

Was Jesus very angry with them?

No, He was as meek as a lamb. He prayed to His Father while He was on the cross. He could not lift up His hands, but He could speak to God. He prayed for these wicked people. He said, 'Father, forgive them, for they know not what they do.'

'Father, forgive,' the sufferer cries,
'Because they know not what they do.'
To heaven He lifts His dying eyes:
Was such a prayer e'er heard below?

Tell me for whom the Saviour prays?
For those who bear Him deadly hate,
Who spat upon His lovely face,
And pierced His blessed hands and feet.

And does the Saviour pray for these?
Ah, then I see that I should pray
For all who hurt me, vex, or tease,
By spiteful things they do or say.

Questions

- Who carried Jesus' cross?
- Could Jesus carry it by Himself?
- Who came after Jesus crying, because He was going to die?
- What did Jesus say to these kind women?
- What did the wicked men do to Jesus when He came to the top of the hill?
- Who took Jesus' clothes?
- Did they tear them all?
- Who did Jesus ask His Father to forgive?
- Should we forgive people who are unkind to us?

Jesus' prayer for those who crucified Him

A verse from the Bible for you to learn

Father, forgive them; for they know not what they do.
Luke 23:34.

LESSON 41

The Cross

PART 2 — LUKE 23:35-43

PONTIUS Pilate wrote these words on the top of Jesus' cross: 'This is the King of the Jews.' But who were the Jews?

The people who lived in Jerusalem were called Jews.

All the wicked people laughed when they read these words. They shook their heads and pouted their lips at Jesus, and said, 'If Thou art the Son of God, come down from the cross.'

Could Jesus have come down?

He could do everything, but He chose to stay to die for His people.

The wicked people said, 'If God loved Him, He would not leave Him to die on the cross.' But His Father let Him die to save people who have sinned.

There was a cross on each side of Jesus, and a thief was nailed to each cross. One of these thieves laughed at Jesus. He said, 'Why dost Thou not save us if Thou art the Son of God?'

The other thief laughed at Jesus too. Then God forgave him for all his sins and made him sorry for them. Then he loved Jesus.

The thief who was sorry said to the other thief, 'We have been wicked; we deserve to be crucified; but Jesus is completely good.' Then he spoke to Jesus and said, 'Remember me when Thou comest into Thy Kingdom.'

And Jesus said, 'You shall be with Me in heaven today.' So Christ heard the poor thief's prayer, for Jesus died so that He might save all who believe that He is the Son of God.

If you go to heaven, you will see that thief.

Upon the hill where Jesus died
A thief was placed on either side,
Each nailed upon a tree.

The one reviled Christ's name in death,
The other cried, with dying breath,
'O Lord, remember me.'

The Saviour heard the poor thief's prayer
And promised He would take him where
Our God and angels dwell.
Alas, his life was spent in sin.
What joy a heaven at last to win
And to escape from hell!

And O, for him what glad surprise,
When heavenly glories met his eyes,
And Christ arrayed in light!
He had just seen the dying pains
That had released his soul from chains
And everlasting night.

Ah, sure, of all the hosts that sing
The praises of their heavenly King,
His voice will loudest sound;
For when just trembling on the brink,
And just about in hell to sink,
Pardon and grace he found.

I would not wish my life to spend,
Like him, a stranger to the Friend
Who died upon the tree;
But yet, like him, whene'er I die,
Let this be my expiring cry,
O Lord, remember me.'

Questions

- What did Pontius Pilate write on the cross?
- Did the wicked people come to see Jesus on the cross?
- What did they say to Jesus?

- Why did Jesus not come down from the cross?
- How many people were crucified with Jesus?
- Did both the thieves go to heaven?
- What did one of the thieves ask Jesus to do?
- Did he ask Jesus to save him from dying on the cross?

We must confess our sins to God

A verse from the Bible for you to learn

If we confess our sins, He is faithful and just to forgive us our sins. l John 1:9.

Lesson 42

The Cross

Part 3 — John 19:25-30. Matthew 27:45-54

JESUS' mother, Mary, stood near the cross. She came to see her Son die. She was very sorry. She felt her heart full of pain at the sight.[1]

She loved her dear, good Son, who had been kind to her ever since He was a baby. He had never done one thing wrong, and she knew He was the Son of God. Jesus was sorry to see His mother's grief.

John had come to the cross, and he was standing near Mary. Jesus wished John to take care of His mother, now that He was going to leave her. So He said to His mother, 'Behold your son!' And He said to John, 'Behold your mother!'

---

[1] 'A sword shall pierce through thy own soul also.' Luke 2:35.

John knew what Jesus meant, and he took Mary to be his mother. So after that Mary always lived with him. Jesus loved His mother, and thought of her even when He was dying.

Jesus was full of pain, and it was very hot. He said, 'I thirst!' The soldiers took a sponge and dipped it in vinegar. Then they put it on a reed and gave it to Jesus.

Jesus just tasted the vinegar and said, 'It is finished!' Then He died. His spirit went to His Father, but His body was still hanging on the cross.

It was three o'clock in the afternoon when Jesus died. He had been nailed to the cross all day. Before Jesus died God had made it very dark, to show He was angry with the wicked people. And God made the earth shake. The people were frightened; and when Jesus was dead, some of them said, 'This must have been the Son of God.'

Mary beholds One dying there,
Whom in her arms she once did bear
And to her bosom press.
On her He casts His pitying eye,
For who should now His place supply,
And cheer her loneliness?

The loving John shall be her son,
And cherish her till life is done,
Within his humble home:
And oft together they shall speak
Of Him who, once despised and weak,
At last in clouds shall come.

O gentle Lord, how great the love,
Which made Thy tender pity move,
Ev'n in the hour of death.
O let me show my parents dear
The same kind love and thoughtful care,
Until their final breath.

Questions

- Where was Jesus' mother, Mary, when He was on the cross?
- Who stood near Mary?
- Who took care of her after Jesus was crucified?
- What did the soldiers give Jesus to drink?
- What did Jesus say just before He died?
- What frightened the people just before He died?

How they treated Christ when He was thirsty on the cross

A verse from the Bible for you to learn

In My thirst they gave Me vinegar to drink. Ps. 69:21.

LESSON 43

The Soldiers

JOHN 19:32-37

AT last the soldiers came to see if Jesus and the two thieves were dead, so that they might bury them before it was dark. The soldiers looked at one thief, and they saw he was not dead. So they broke his legs, and that killed him. Then they looked at the other thief, and they saw he was not dead. So they broke his legs too.

Then they looked at Jesus. They saw He was dead, so they did not break His legs. But one of the soldiers took a long stick with a sharp point at the end, called a spear, and put it in His side. And out of Jesus' side blood and water came flowing out onto the ground. John was standing nearby, and he saw the blood.

Do you remember how Jesus, at supper the night before, had poured wine into a cup and said to the disciples, 'This is My blood, which is shed for many'?

Now His blood was poured out. The spear made a hole in Jesus' side. There was a hole in His side, and a hole in each hand, and a hole in each foot, and His forehead was pricked with thorns, and His eyes had shed many tears, and blood had come from His skin. All this He suffered for people who have sinned, just like we have, so that God might forgive them their sins.[1]

'Yes, He is surely dead,'
The cruel soldier said,
Then pierced the Saviour's side.
Behold, a mingled tide
Of blood and water, flowing from the wound,
Covers with crimson stains Golgotha's ground!

The loving John was near;
He saw the soldier's spear
Bring forth that wondrous flood
Of water and of blood;
And well remembered how his Master said,
He came for sinful man His blood to shed.

The blood that flowed that day
Long since has passed away;
But still there flows a stream,
Though by all eyes unseen,
For those that trust the blood on Calvary spilt;
And in that stream their souls are washed from guilt.

---

[1] 'In whom we have redemption through His blood, the forgiveness of sins, according to the riches of His grace' Eph. 1:7

And does it flow for me?
And can I washed be?
For oft my soul has been
Spotted and stained with sin.
Mercy I ask, because the Saviour died;
And thus, as by a stream, be purified.

Questions

- How did the soldiers kill the thieves?
- Why did they kill them so soon?
- Why did the soldiers not break Jesus' legs?
- What did they put into Jesus' side?
- What is a spear?
- What came out of His side?
- What had Jesus poured out once at supper, when He said, 'This is My blood'?
- Why did Jesus shed His blood on the cross?

What takes away sin?

A verse from the Bible for you to learn

The blood of Jesus Christ His Son cleanseth us from all sin.
1 John 1:7.

Lesson 44

The Grave

John 19:38-42. Luke 23:55, 56. Matthew 27:60

There was one rich man who loved Jesus; his name was Joseph (not Mary's husband; this was another Joseph). Joseph had a garden, and in the garden he had a grave. Perhaps he meant to be buried there himself when he died.

But now Joseph thought, 'I should like to put the Lord Jesus in my grave.' It was a very nice grave, and no one had ever been put there yet.

So Joseph went to Pontius Pilate and said, 'I want the dead body of Jesus. May I take it down from the cross, and keep it myself?'

And Pilate said, 'Yes, you may have it.'

Then Joseph was glad. He brought some nice, white, clean linen.

What do you think that was for?

To wrap Jesus in. And he brought some spices (sweet-smelling things from plants). Nicodemus came with him, and they took the nails out of Jesus' hands and feet, and took his body down from the cross. Then Joseph wrapped a cloth round His head, and another cloth round His waist, and he put sweet spices on Him. Then some men carried Jesus along to Joseph's garden.

In the garden there was a large rock, and a hole in the rock, like a hole in the wall. They walked into this large dark hole, and they laid Jesus down alone. Now He was at rest; He felt no pain or sorrow. The wicked people were not near; and there lay the Lord in His quiet grave. The men took a very large stone and stopped up the hole, so that nobody could come in. No beast or bird could touch the Lord Jesus. There were trees and flowers near Him in this nice garden. There were angels there watching over Him, though no one could see them.

Where were the women who loved Jesus?

They had been looking at Him on the cross. How they must have cried when they saw Him bleed, and when they heard Him cry out to God!

The women had seen Joseph and Nicodemus take down the body from the cross. They had followed the men into the garden. They had seen it put so carefully into the grave.

They said to each other, 'Let us get more spices, and make sweet ointment to put on the Lord Jesus.' Joseph had put some spices on Jesus' body, but they wanted to put more spices on it. So they went home and made nice ointment.

Questions

- Who put Jesus into his own grave?
- Where was the grave?
- Who did Joseph ask when he wanted Jesus' body?
- What did Joseph wrap it in?
- What did he put round Jesus' head and waist?
- What was put in front of the grave?
- Did anyone see where Jesus was laid?
- What did the women make when they went home?

What happened to Jesus' body after He was crucified?

A verse from the Bible for you to learn

And when Joseph had taken the body, he wrapped it in a clean linen cloth, and laid it in his own new tomb.
Matt. 27:59, 60.

Lesson 45

The Resurrection

Mark 16:1-6. Luke 24:3-10. Matthew 28:9, 10

One morning very early, when Jesus had been dead only two days, the women came into the garden. It was not yet quite light, for the sun was just rising.

As the women walked along with their ointment they said to each other, 'How shall we get into the grave? The men put a large stone in front of it, and the stone is so big that we cannot roll it away.' The women did not know what to do.

At last, when they came to the grave, they found that the stone was rolled away already. The women were quite surprised. Then they were afraid that some wicked people had rolled it away and stolen the body of Jesus. This made them very sad. They looked into the grave, and saw that Jesus was not there.

But soon they saw two beautiful angels standing by them. Their faces were bright like the sun, their clothes whiter than snow.

The women trembled when they saw the angels; but the angels spoke sweetly and kindly to them, saying, 'Do not be afraid; we know that you are looking for Jesus. He is not here now; He is alive. Do you not remember how He said that He would come to life again after He had been crucified?'

'Come,' said the angels, 'and look at the place where Jesus lay. Run quickly, and tell His disciples that Jesus is alive, and that they shall see Him very soon.'

The women were very glad indeed. They ran as quickly as they could to tell the disciples. But as they were running, who do you think they saw?

It was Jesus Himself! He did not look as He once had looked. There were no tears on His cheeks; they were all wiped away.[1]

---

[1] 'Thou hast made Him exceeding glad with Thy countenance.' Ps. 21:6.

He was not weak and faint as when He carried His cross. He could never die again.[2]

How pleased the women were to see Him! They knelt down on the ground and held His feet, so that He might not go away. They called Him their Lord and their God. Still they felt a little afraid, but Jesus told them not to be afraid.

Jesus said, 'Go, tell My brothers that I shall soon see them again.'

Whom did Jesus call His brothers?

His disciples. He had forgiven them for having run away when the wicked men took Him.

The women ran, as Jesus had told them, to the disciples. They said, 'We have seen angels! We have seen the Lord Jesus! He is walking about, and you will see Him soon.' But the disciples would not believe the women.

Behold, how swift those women fly!
Both fear and joy are in their eye.
Ah, sure they've seen some glorious thing,
Or haste some glorious news to bring.

An angel's voice they have just heard;
To them the Lord has just appeared;
With fear their hearts are beating fast;
With joy the news to tell they haste.

They once wept with their dying Lord;
Now to their eyes He is restored.
He for their sakes has shed His blood,
And now is proved the Son of God.

I wonder not their joy is great,
For what could greater joy create?
Have they not found that matchless Friend,
On whom their hopes for heaven depend?

---

[2] 'Christ being raised from the dead dieth no more.' Rom. 6:9.

Questions

- When did the women come to the grave?
- Why did they come?
- Who rolled away the large stone?
- How did the angels look?
- Were the women pleased when they saw them?
- What did the angels tell the women?
- Who did the women run to tell what they had seen?
- Who did the women see as they went along?
- What did the women do when they saw Jesus?
- Did Jesus forgive His disciples for having left Him alone?
- Did the disciples believe that the women had seen Jesus?

Christ's words after He rose from the dead

A verse from the Bible for you to learn

I am He that liveth, and was dead; and, behold, I am alive for evermore. Rev. 1:18.

LESSON 46

Mary Magdalene

JOHN 20:1-19

I HAVE told you of two Marys: Mary, the mother of Jesus, and another Mary, the sister of Lazarus. But there was still another, called Mary Magdalene. She came very early to the grave of Jesus, before the other women came. She looked into the grave, but saw no angels. So she came running back and told

Peter and John that Jesus was not in His grave. 'I am afraid,' said Mary Magdalene, 'that some wicked people have taken Him away, and that we shall not be able to find Him.'

So Peter and John began to run as fast as they could, but John ran the faster and he came first to the grave. He stooped down and peeped in, and he saw the clothes lying in the grave. Soon afterwards Peter came and went down into the grave. He saw the clothes neatly folded, and the cloth that was round Jesus' head lying in a place by itself. Then John went in too, and he remembered what Jesus had said about being alive again.

'It is all true,' thought John, 'He is alive and has left His grave.'

Then Peter and John came out of the grave and went to their own house. But they saw no angels, nor did they see Jesus.

Where was Mary Magdalene all this time?

She was standing crying near the grave. She was alone, because Peter and John had gone home.

At last she stooped down and looked into the grave, and she saw a beautiful sight: two angels. One of them was sitting where Jesus' head had been, and the other where His feet had been!

The angels said to Mary, 'Why are you crying?' But still she went on crying; she said, 'Some people have taken away the Lord Jesus, and I cannot find Him.'

When she had said this, she heard a man behind her saying, 'Why are you crying?'

She did not know who it was that spoke to her. She thought it might be the gardener. She thought this man might have taken away the body of Jesus. She wanted to know where the man had put the body so that she could take it away.

The man said 'Mary!' She knew that voice and, turning round, she looked and saw that it was Jesus. How glad she was to see her Lord and Master, whom she loved!

But Jesus could not stay with her. He told her to go and tell His dear disciples that He was alive. 'I am soon going up to My Father in heaven, but I shall see My disciples first.'

Mary Magdalene came and told the disciples. They were all crying, but they would not believe what Mary said.

Mary was glad that she had gone to look for Jesus. She was the first of all the people who saw Jesus after He was alive again.[1]

And why is Mary full of fears?
Her eye, why so bedimmed with tears
While gazing on that grave?
She cannot find the body there
Of One who lives, who's standing near,
Whose arm from death can save.

'Why weepest thou?' the Saviour cries.
'I've lost my Lord,' she quick replies,
And thinks not it is He.
He speaks again. His voice she knows;
And now her heart with joy o'erflows
Her dearest Lord to see.

His body dead she once had sought
Within the tomb, and little thought
Of this supreme delight.
Oh, vain were all her anxious fears,
And vain were all her bitter tears,
That flowed both day and night.

And is not He for ever near,
Although His voice we cannot hear,
Or see His glorious face?
Yes, over us His wings are spread,
And blessings still are gently shed,
For He fills every place.

---

[1] 'He appeared first to Mary Magdalene.' Mark 16:9.

Questions

- How many Marys have I told you about?
- Who came very early to the grave of Jesus?
- Which two disciples ran to the grave of Jesus?
- Who came there first?
- Which of them went into the grave first?
- What did Peter and John see in the grave?
- Did John believe that Jesus was alive again?
- Did Peter and John see Jesus in the grave?
- Who did they see in the grave?
- Who stood alone, crying, near the grave?
- What did she see when she looked in?
- Why did Mary Magdalene cry?
- Who was the man who spoke to her kindly?
- Was He the gardener?
- Did Jesus stay with Mary?
- Who was the first person that saw Jesus after He was alive again?

The happiness of the righteous

A verse from the Bible for you to learn

Be glad in the Lord, and rejoice, ye righteous. Ps. 32:11.

LESSON 47

The Two Friends

LUKE 24:13-48

IT was early in the morning when the women went to look for Jesus. In the evening two good men were walking together into the country. As they walked, they talked about Jesus. They had not seen Him since He was alive again. They did not even know that He was alive. They talked about Him dying on the cross. It made them very sad to speak about it.

At last a man came and spoke to them. They thought He was a stranger; yet He seemed to be a kind man.

He said, 'Why do you cry? I see you are talking about something very sad.'

'Yes,' said these good men, 'we are talking of something sad. Did you never hear of Jesus? Did you never hear what wonderful things He did: how He cured blind and dumb and sick people, and how He taught people about God'? And all the people loved Him; but at last He was crucified. We thought He was the Son of God, but now we are afraid He was not, because He is dead. And we are afraid that we shall never see Him again.'

The kind stranger was sorry to see these good men cry. He began to talk to them, and to tell them that Jesus was the Son of God, and that He had been crucified to save people from their sins. So He must rise again and go back to His Father.

This kind stranger said a great deal more. He knew all the verses in the Bible, and told these men many things they did not know. They liked listening to the stranger; they did not feel so sad while He was talking.

At last these men came to their own house. It was in the country. The stranger seemed as if He was going on farther; but the two good men said to Him, 'Stay at our house; it is getting dark. Come and eat with us, and sleep here. Do come in.'

Then the stranger said that He would come in.

The men went into a room, and there they had supper. They all three sat down together round the table. The stranger took some bread and broke it and began to pray to God. Then the two men found out who the stranger was.

'It is the Lord!' they cried. And so it was. They looked towards Him, but they could see Him no more. He did not open the door, but yet He had gone.

Then the men thought of all that Jesus had said. 'How sweetly He talked to us!' they said. 'Did we not feel our hearts quite warm while He was speaking to us about the Bible, and telling us its meaning?'

Do you think these men went to bed that night?

O no! They could not sleep. 'Let us go,' they said, 'and tell the disciples that we have seen Jesus.' So they left their supper and set out in the night to walk back to Jerusalem. They walked quickly and soon came to the city.

The disciples were all shut up together in a room. They had locked the doors to prevent the wicked people getting in, but they let these good men come in. The disciples were at supper.

'We have seen Jesus,' said these good men, 'He walked with us and talked with us, but we did not know Him till He sat down with us at supper and broke some bread and gave thanks to His Father.' The disciples said, 'Some women have seen Him, and Peter has seen Him.'

But, while they were eating their supper and talking about Jesus, they looked and saw Jesus standing in the middle of the room. Though the door was locked, He had come in. How do you think the disciples felt?

They were frightened: they could not believe that it was indeed Jesus Himself.

Jesus spoke kindly to them. 'Why are you afraid?' He asked. Then He said, 'Look at My hands and feet. It is I Myself.' Then Jesus showed His disciples the marks that the nails had made in His hands and feet, and the hole that the spear had made in His side.

Then the disciples saw that it was their own dear Master. They were glad, very glad to see Him. They had been crying ever since they had lost Him. They saw that He had forgiven them for having run away. He said nothing to them about it. He had even forgiven Peter. He knew that Peter loved Him, and that he was very sorry.

The disciples were so surprised to see Jesus that they could hardly believe He was alive. Jesus knew that they did not quite believe, so He said, 'Have you anything to eat?' Then the disciples gave Him a piece of fish and some honey from their supper. Jesus took the food and began to eat, so that the disciples might see that He really was alive.

Then afterwards He talked to them and told them why He had died, and that He was going back to His father to pray for them.

That was a pleasant night for the poor disciples. It was not like that sad night when Jesus was so sorrowful in the garden. His sorrows were over, and He would never feel pain again any more.

There are but three around that table met.
It's their last meal, for now the sun has set.
One breaks the bread. I know that lovely face,
That voice, but lo, He's vanished from the place!

'Was it an angel? No, it was the Lord;
He lives again. He is to us restored.'
What joy now fills these hearts that once were filled
With fears! Ah, now for ever, ever stilled!

'Well might our hearts burn in us by the way
While Jesus spake,' the fond disciples say;
'How sweet was His discourse! We little thought
That it was He. How strange we knew Him not.

But stranger far that we did not believe
That He would rise again! Could He deceive?
O no; He is the faithful and the true,
And what He says He evermore will do.'

Questions

- On what day did Jesus come out of His grave?
- What were two good men doing that evening?
- What were they talking about?
- Who came and walked with them?
- Did they know that Jesus was with them?
- What did Jesus talk to them about?
- Did Jesus come into the house of the two good men?
- When did they find out who He was?
- Did Jesus stay in the room?
- Did the good men stay in their own house that night?
- Where did they go?
- Who came into the room although the door was locked?
- What did Jesus show to all His disciples?
- Were the disciples sure that Jesus was the same Jesus?
- What did Jesus eat?

How Jesus made His disciples know Him again after He rose again

A verse from the Bible for you to learn

He showed unto them His hands and His side. Then were the disciples glad, when they saw the Lord. John 20:20.

Lesson 48

Thomas

John 20:24-31

You have heard how the disciples saw Jesus in the evening. But one of the disciples was not there when Jesus came. His name was Thomas. I do not know why he was not there.

When the disciples saw Thomas next, they said to him, 'We have seen Jesus. On the Lord's Day night we saw Him. He came into the room as we were sitting together, and He spoke to us. We are sure it was Jesus Himself, because He showed us the marks of the nails in His hands and feet, and the hole in His side where the spear went in.'

But Thomas would not believe the disciples. He said, 'I do not think you saw Jesus Himself. He died on the cross. I never will believe unless I put my fingers into the marks of the nails, and put my hand into the hole in His side.'

It was very wrong of Thomas to speak in this way. He should have remembered that Jesus had promised to come alive again.

Jesus heard Thomas speak, though Thomas could not see Him. But Jesus was always with the disciples, and heard all they said because He is God.

Next Lord's Day evening the disciples were in a room together. Thomas was there too. The doors were locked to keep the wicked people out, but the disciples knew that Jesus could come in. And He did come. They saw Him standing in the middle of the room. He spoke kindly to them and said, 'Peace be unto you!'

Then He spoke to Thomas. 'Come,' He said to Thomas, 'here are My hands. Put your finger into the marks. And here is the hole in My side; put your hand into it.'

Now Thomas knew that Jesus had heard him speak so sinfully, and he felt ashamed and sorry.

He saw that it was Jesus Himself, and he cried out, 'My Lord and my God!'

Then Jesus said to Thomas, 'Now, because you have seen, you believe. Blessed are they who have not seen, and yet have believed.' Jesus forgave Thomas for what he had said. Thomas really loved Jesus.

Questions

- Which of the disciples would not believe that Jesus was alive again?
- What did Jesus say he must do before he would believe?
- When did Thomas see Jesus again?
- What did Jesus say to him when He saw him?
- Did Thomas then believe that Jesus was alive?

How God always hears us speak

A verse from the Bible for you to learn

There is not a word in my tongue, but, lo, O Lord, Thou knowest it altogether. Ps. 139:4.

LESSON 49

The Dinner

JOHN 20:1-19

JESUS told His disciples to go far away into the country, and He said, 'I will come and see you again.'

So the disciples went away from Jerusalem, and they went into the country. They came to the place where they had once lived beside the sea. They had some ships on the water. They used them when they were fishing.

One night Peter said to the disciples, 'I shall go and fish'. The other disciples said, 'We will go with you.' So they got into a ship, and all night long they tried to catch fish, but they could not catch any. So in the morning they were tired and hungry.

They looked up and saw a man standing on the shore. They did not know who the man was. The man called out to them and said, 'Children, have you anything to eat?'

The poor disciples said, 'No.' They had caught no fish all night.

The man said, 'Let down your net on the right side of the ship and you shall find some fish.'

They did as the man told them, and they caught so many fish in the net that they could hardly lift it out of the water.

Now John found out who the man was. He said to Peter, 'It is the Lord.' Peter was very glad, and he jumped into the water, and swam first to Jesus. The other disciples came soon afterwards in their little ship, with their nets and their fish.

Jesus knew that they were tired and hungry. By the shore there was a fire, and some fish on the fire and some bread. How kind it was of Jesus to give food to His poor hungry disciples!

Jesus said to them, 'Bring some of the fishes that you have caught.' So Peter went and took up the net and found it full of big fish - one hundred and fifty three. This was one of Jesus' great miracles.

Then said Jesus to the disciples, 'Come and dine.' So they all sat down to dine together. Then Jesus took the bread, and gave some to each of them. He took the fish and gave some of it to them too.

Now the disciples were quite sure that it was Jesus who was feeding them. This was the way they used to dine together before Jesus had died. Now He was alive again, and they dined together once more. But they knew He was not going to stay long with them.

When they had all finished eating, Jesus said to Peter, 'Do you love Me?'

Peter said, 'Yes, Lord; Thou knowest that I love Thee.'

Then Jesus said, 'Feed My lambs,' (that is, 'Teach other people more about Me').

Peter did love Jesus, and Jesus knew he did. Yet Jesus said again, 'Do you love Me?'

Peter said again, 'Lord, Thou knowest that I love Thee.'

Then Jesus said, 'Feed My sheep.'

Jesus asked Peter the same thing once more: 'Do you love Me?'

Peter was afraid Jesus did not believe him, and this made him sorry. He said, 'Lord, Thou knowest everything. Thou knowest that I love Thee.'

Jesus said again, 'Feed My sheep.'

If Peter loved Jesus he would do what Jesus told him, and go and teach people.

Do you love Jesus, children? What would you answer if Jesus said to you, 'Do you love Me?' Could you say to Jesus, 'Look into My heart, and Thou wilt see that I love Thee?' If you do really love Him, you will hate lies and a bad temper, and you will try to be kind and gentle, and to please Jesus all the day.

Why did Jesus ask Peter so often whether he loved Him? Why did He ask him three times over?

Peter had said three times over that he did not know Jesus. So Jesus wanted to hear him say he loved Him three times over.

Then Jesus told Peter what would happen to him when he was old. Jesus said to Peter, 'When you were young, you walked about where you liked; but when you are old, some men will take you, and stretch out your hands and carry you where you do not want to go.'

Jesus meant that Peter would be crucified. Men would stretch out his hands on a cross, and nail him, as they had done to Jesus. Wicked people would crucify Peter because he loved Jesus, but Peter would never say again that he did not know Jesus.

Peter was not proud now, as he used to be. And Peter would pray to God to keep him from sin.

Death has not changed the Saviour's heart.
Behold those pierced hands give out
The food they have prepared;
While seven disciples sit around,
Joying that they the Friend have found
For whom they fondly cared,

Found Him as ready to forgive
As when with them He used to live
Before His cruel death;
For they had fled when He was tried,
And Peter had His Lord denied
With most unfaithful breath.

The Lord well knew that love inspired
His bosom, yet three times inquired,
'Simon, dost thou love Me?'
And Peter said, 'O Thou alone,
To whom all things are fully known,
Thou knowest that I love Thee.'

And by what sign his faithful love
Shall Peter to his Saviour prove?
'O feed My lambs and sheep!'
And gladly this will Peter do,
That others may be pardoned too,
And taught from sin to keep.

O happy they who truly can
Entreat the Lord their heart to scan
And see their faithful love!
And happy they who still obey
His sweet commands, and what they say
By faithful actions prove.

Questions

- Did the disciples stay in Jerusalem, or did they go into the country?
- Why did they go out in boats one night?
- Could they catch any fish?
- Who spoke to them in the morning?
- What did He tell them to do?
- Which of the disciples knew first that it was Jesus speaking to them?
- Which of them jumped into the water and swam to Jesus?
- What did the disciples find ready for them when they were come to Jesus?
- Had they caught any fish in the net?
- What question did Jesus ask Peter three times?
- What did Jesus want Peter to do, if he really loved Him?
- How can children show that they really love Jesus?
- What did Jesus tell Peter that wicked men would do to him one day?

Who loves Christ, and who does not

A verse from the Bible for you to learn

If a man love Me, he will keep My words. . . . He that loveth Me not keepeth not My sayings. John 14:23, 24.

Lesson 50

The Ascension

Matthew 28:16-20, Luke 24:46-53, Acts 1:4-14

Jesus used to come and see His disciples after He was made alive again. But He did not stay with them for long.

He told them He was soon going up to His Father. 'When I am gone, you must tell people about Me. You must tell the people who crucified Me that I will forgive them if they will believe on Me. The Holy Spirit will come down from heaven, for My Father has promised to send Him down soon. Wait at Jerusalem till He comes. I will always be with you, though you do not see Me. Some day I shall come back again.'

The disciples asked Jesus when He would come back, but Jesus would not tell them.

One day Jesus and His disciples walked together to the top of a hill. Jesus began to pray with His disciples and He lifted up His hands and blessed them. While He was doing this, He was taken up to heaven, and a cloud hid Him at last from the eyes of His disciples.

They still looked up and saw the cloud go higher and higher till they could see it no more. But still they went on looking. Then they heard some persons speaking to them. When they looked to see who it was, they saw two angels standing beside them.

The angels were dressed in white shining clothes. They said, 'Why do you look so long at the sky? Jesus will come again some day.' The disciples then went back to Jerusalem to wait for the Holy Spirit.

Perhaps you think they were very unhappy, now that Jesus was gone? No, they were not. They knew He had gone to get a place in heaven ready for them, and that they would live with Him there for ever. This made them glad.

Questions

- Can you tell me a verse about loving Jesus?
- Did Jesus live always with His disciples after He was alive again, or did He only come to see them sometimes?
- What did Jesus tell His disciples to do when He went back to His Father?
- Did He tell them when He would come back?
- What was Jesus doing just before He went away in the cloud?
- Who spoke to the disciples as they were looking at the cloud?
- Were the disciples unhappy when Jesus was gone?
- Why were they not unhappy?

How Jesus left His disciples, after He had risen from the dead

A verse from the Bible for you to learn

And it came to pass, while He blessed them, He was parted from them, and carried up into heaven. Luke 24:51.

LESSON 51

Peter in Prison

ACTS 2:12:1-23

WHO had Jesus promised to send when He went to His Father?

The Holy Spirit.

And He did send the Holy Spirit, as He promised. Then the disciples began to speak of Jesus to all the wicked people. They said to them, 'You have crucified the Son of God. He is alive, and has gone up to sit on His Father's throne. If you believe on Him, He will forgive you and give you the Holy Spirit.'

Some of the wicked people were sorry for what they had done to Jesus, and begged God to forgive them. But some of the wicked people were not sorry, and they tried to kill the disciples.

A wicked king caught James and cut off his head with a sword. Then he shut up Peter in prison. He was going to kill him too.

Have you ever seen a prison? It is a dark place, with great doors and bars, and walls all round it.

Some soldiers took Peter and put chains on his hands and chains on his feet. Then they locked the door of the prison. Some soldiers sat at the door so that no one could get in.

Peter's friends were very unhappy because he was in prison, but they could not take him out. Yet there was one thing they could do; they could pray to God to save Peter, and so they did. Peter's friends sat up at night and prayed to God.

The wicked king said, 'Tomorrow I shall have Peter killed.' But God would not let Peter be killed. So God told one of His beautiful angels to go and let Peter out of the prison. The angel could go into the prison without opening the doors.

It was night when the angel came. Peter was asleep. On each side of him there was a soldier, and Peter was chained to them both. You would not like to sleep in a prison with soldiers near you, and chains on your hands. But Peter knew that God loved him, and that he was safe.

So the angel came. It was dark in the prison.

Could Peter see the angel?

Yes; for the angel was bright like the sun, and made the prison light.

The angel touched Peter on the side and lifted him up. At once the chains fell off Peter's hands and feet. He told Peter to put on his clothes, and Peter did so.

Then the angel said, 'Follow me.' So the angel walked out first, and Peter followed him. They went through the prison.

But the men at the doors did not see Peter go out, because God made them sleep.

Peter was quite surprised; he thought he was dreaming and that he did not see a real angel.

At last Peter came to a big iron gate. It was locked, but the angel did not need a key to open it. It opened itself, and Peter and the angel could go through it.

Now they were in the street. Still the angel went on, and Peter came after him. But they did not speak a word.

All the people were asleep, and did not know that a bright angel was walking in the street. The angel only walked down one street. Then he went back to heaven and left Peter standing alone in the street, in the dark.

Peter stood some time thinking to himself, 'What a wonderful thing has happened! I was shut up in prison, but God has sent His angel to let me out. The king meant to kill me tomorrow, but now I shall not be killed.' I know that Peter thanked God for His kindness.

Peter did not stay all night in the street. He went to the house of a good woman he knew, and he knocked at the door. Were the people in the house asleep?

No, they were all awake, though it was night.

Why were they not in bed?

This good woman had heard how the king was going to kill Peter the next day. So she and her friends were praying for Peter. While they were praying they heard a knock. It was a strange thing to hear a knock in the night, but they never guessed who it was.

A maid named Rhoda went to the door. But she did not open it. She heard Peter speak, and how happy she was! She knew his voice. She did not say, 'Are you Peter?' She was sure it was Peter. She was so much surprised that she forgot to open the door; but ran back to the good woman and the rest of the disciples. She told them, 'Peter is standing at the gate!'

But they said, 'No, it cannot be Peter. He is shut up in prison.'

The maid said, 'It is Peter. I am sure it is.'

While they were talking, Peter was standing outside. And he went on knocking, because nobody opened the door. Soon his friends ran and opened the door, and when they saw Peter they were very surprised.

'How did you get out of prison?' they asked him.

Then Peter made a sign with his hand so that they would all be quiet. Then he told them how he got out of prison.

'God sent an angel,' said Peter, 'who brought me out of the prison. Go and tell all my friends what has happened, for I must go away.' So Peter went and hid himself in a place where the wicked king could not find him.

What do you think the soldiers said when they could not find Peter in the morning?

They were very frightened. They saw his chains, but they did not see Peter. They found the gates locked. They could not think how Peter got out of prison.

So the king sent for Peter. This was the day when Peter was to be killed. All the wicked people in Jerusalem were expecting to see him. The king's servants asked, 'Where is Peter? Bring him out.'

The soldiers answered. 'We cannot tell where Peter is. He is not here.'

The servants went and told the king that Peter was not in the prison. The king was very angry. He said, 'Bring the soldiers to me. They must have fallen asleep.'

When the soldiers came, they could not tell the king how Peter got away. But you know why. God made them sleep when the angel came for Peter. The king was in a great rage and said, 'The soldiers must be killed.'

What a wicked king this was! He loved to do wickedness. He was very proud. He hated God and God's people. He only cared to please himself. At last God sent an angel to kill him, and worms ate up his flesh until he died.

God sends angels to punish the wicked, and to help people like Peter, who love Him.

'Awake!' the angel cries; and from the hands
Of wondering Peter fall the iron bands;
The gates fly open of their own accord,
And Peter is to liberty restored.

His guide he follows through the gloom of night
(Where angels are, there needs no other light)
The angel's gone, and Peter, left alone,
Sees and admires the love His God has shown.

At yonder gate he knocks, whence prayer ascends.
On this sad night from Peter's sorrowing friends;
With glad surprise the maiden hears his voice.
All round him flock, and with one heart rejoice.

Questions

- What did the disciples tell the wicked people in Jerusalem?
- Were any of the wicked people who had killed Jesus sorry for their wickedness?
- What happened to James at last?
- Where was Peter shut up?
- What were Peter's friends doing for him when he was in prison?
- Who came to Peter one night?
- How did Peter get out from his chains?
- How did he get through the big doors?
- Where did the angel leave Peter standing alone?
- Where did Peter go then?
- What were the people in the house doing when Peter knocked?
- How did Rhoda know it was Peter knocking?
- Why did she not open the door?

- What did Peter tell all the friends when he had made them quiet?
- Where did Peter go then?
- Why were the soldiers frightened in the morning?
- Why did the wicked king send for Peter?
- What did the king want to do to the soldiers?
- How did God punish this wicked king at last?

How the righteous are saved from danger

A verse from the Bible for you to learn

The angel of the Lord encampeth round about them that fear Him, and delivereth them. Ps. 34:7.

Lesson 52

John

Revelation 1:9-19; 4:1-5; 22

Almost all the twelve disciples were killed by wicked men. When Peter was old, some wicked men crucified him because he loved Jesus. Now he is in heaven with Jesus, clothed in a white robe, and all his tears wiped away. His dear Lord Jesus is always near him, and this makes Peter happy.

John lived till he was very, very old indeed. A wicked king caught him, and put him on an island far away from his friends. There was water all around, so he could not get away.

Was John unhappy there?

No. God was with him, and John loved to think of the Father and of His Son Jesus.

It was the Lord's Day, and John was thinking about God. John heard a voice behind him like the noise of a trumpet, very loud indeed.

He turned round to see who it was. Who do you think he saw?

It was the Lord Jesus come down from the heaven, all glorious and shining! When John saw Him he could not speak or stand. John was afraid, and he fell down on the ground as if he was dead. But Jesus touched him with His hand and said, 'Fear not; I am He that liveth and was dead, and behold, I am alive for evermore.' Then Jesus took John up into heaven, and an angel showed him most beautiful things.

John saw a throne on which God sat. There was a rainbow round the throne. There were many, many seats there. Men were sitting on them, all clothed in white, with crowns of gold on their heads. The men took off their crowns and threw them down before the throne and praised Jesus, the Lamb of God.

John saw many angels, more than he could count, standing round the throne, singing praises to the Lamb. But of all the things John saw in heaven, there was nothing so glorious as God himself.

In heaven there is no sun or moon or candle or lamp. Yet it is always bright, because God shines more brightly than the sun. The music of harps and sweet singing is always to be heard, for all the angels can sing the praises of God.

John wondered at the things he saw and heard, and he fell down at the feet of the angel who had shown them to him. But the angel said, 'You must not worship me; I am only a servant of God. You must worship God.'

Then the angel went on speaking and said, 'Jesus will soon come down from heaven to judge the world. He will open the gates of heaven to let those people in who love God's Word. But those who tell lies, and do wicked things, shall be shut out.' All the people who love Jesus will see Him come again in the clouds.

Do you wish to see Jesus, my little children?

Then you may answer, 'Even so, come Lord Jesus.' And I hope that when you die your spirit will go to Jesus, and that when Jesus comes again He will bring you with Him.

John wrote down in a book the things he saw in heaven. All that John wrote is in the Bible.

At last John died, and his soul went to God. He is with Jesus now in heaven. He is now playing on a golden harp and singing with the angels. But, when Jesus comes again in the clouds, John will come with Him. [1]

When John was by the angel led
To the bright world on high,
He saw what joys await the dead
When up to heaven they fly.

He saw them round the Father's throne,
Gazing upon His face,
Singing with harps of sweetest tone
The praises of His grace.

He saw them clothed in robes of white,
Such as the angels wear,
Shining like stars of morning, bright,
And like the angels fair.

He saw the city where they dwelt,
Whose praises can't be told.
The walls of precious stones were built,
The streets were purest gold.

He saw the Lamb whose blood was spilt
To give His people rest;
With His bright beams the place was filled,
And every heart was blest.

---

[1] 'Them also which sleep in Jesus will God bring with Him.' 1 Thess. 4:14.

Charmed with the sight, John bent his knee
Before that angel fair,
Who said, 'You must not worship me.
To God address your prayer.'

It's God who rules the angel host
In the fair world of light;
It's God who shuts the spirits lost
In realms of endless night.

O let me then this God implore
To pardon all my sin,
And open to me the heavenly door,
And bid me enter in.

Questions

- Where was John shut up alone?
- Who came to see John when he was alone?
- What did Jesus show him?
- Who did he see sitting round God's throne?
- How many angels did he see?
- What makes heaven always light?
- When John fell down at the angel's feet, what did the angel say?
- What will Jesus do when He comes again?
- Who wrote down in a book about heaven and the angels?

Christ shall come again

A verse from the Bible for you to learn

Behold, He cometh with clouds; and every eye shall see Him, and they also which pierced Him. Rev. 1:7.

Lesson 53

The Judgement Day

1 Thessalonians 4:15-17, Revelation 20:11-15

You know that Jesus will come again in the clouds? Children, do you know when He will come? Shall I tell you when Jesus will come?

You would like to know, but I cannot tell you when He will come because I do not know. The angels do not know what day it will be. No one knows but God.[1] There will be many wicked people in the world then, and some good people.[2] An angel will blow a great trumpet, and Jesus will say to the people who are dead, 'Come out of your graves!'

The bodies of all the dead people will come out of their graves.[3] Those who love Christ will be like the angels and will fly up into the air. Those who love God and are alive when Jesus comes, He will take up into the air to meet Him. As soon as they see Jesus, they will be like Him, all shining and glorious.

Jesus will sit upon a white throne, and everybody will stand round His throne. He will open some books, in which He has written down all the things that everybody has done. God has seen all the bad things you have done. He can see in the dark as well as in the light, and He knows all your sinful thoughts.

He will read out of His books all the bad things that those people have done who do not love God, and the angels too will be standing round the throne to hear. Yet God will forgive many people because Christ died on the cross.

---

[1] 'But of that day and hour knoweth no man, no, not the angels of heaven, but My Father only.' Matt. 24:36.

[2] 'Nevertheless, when the Son of man cometh, shall He find faith on the earth?' Luke 18:8. 'So shall it be at the end of the world: the angels shall come forth, and sever the wicked from among the just.' Matt. 13:49

[3] 'The hour is coming, in the which all that are in the graves shall hear His voice, and shall come forth.' John 5:28, 29.

Who will He forgive?

He will forgive those who love Jesus with all their hearts.[4] He has written down their names in another book, called 'The Book of Life.' He forgives their sins, He will wipe away their tears and He will let them live with Him for ever.

Do you hope that Jesus has written down your name in His book?

So you must ask Him to give you His Holy Spirit. Then you will love Jesus, and you will hate to do what is wrong.[5]

But what will God do to those who do not love Him? God will bind them in chains, and put them in a lake of fire. There they will gnash their teeth and weep and wail for ever.[6]

God will put Satan in the same place, and all the devils.[7] Satan is the father of the wicked, and he and his children shall be tormented for ever. They shall not have one drop of water to cool their burning tongues.

Many people in hell will say, 'How I wish I had listened to what I learned from the Bible! But I would not think about them. Now it is too late. I never can come out of this dreadful place. How foolish I have been! There was a time when God would have heard my prayers, but now I weep and wail in vain.'[8]

I hope, my dear children, that none of you will ever speak such sad words. Remember that Satan goes about as a cunning serpent, trying to make you disobey God. But Christ will keep you from wickedness if you pray to Him.

---

[4] 'The kingdom which he hath promised to them that love Him.' James 2:5.

[5] 'If any man love not the Lord Jesus Christ, let him be Anathema Maranatha' (or accursed). 1 Cor. 16:22.

[6] 'Bind him hand and foot, and take him away, and cast him into outer darkness; there shall be weeping and gnashing of teeth.' Matt. 22:13.

[7] 'Depart from me, ye cursed, into everlasting fire, prepared for the devil and his angels.' Matt. 25:41.

[8] 'And thou mourn at the last, when thy flesh and thy body are consumed, and say, How have I hated instruction, and my heart despised reproof; and have not obeyed the voice of my teachers!' Prov. 5:11-13.

One day God will burn up this world we live in. It is dreadful to see a house on fire. Did you ever see one? But how dreadful it will be to see this great world and all the houses and trees burning! The noise will be terrible. The heat will be very great.[9] The wicked will not be able to get away. They will be cast into the lake of fire.[10]

If you are God's child, you will not be frightened when the world is burning. You will be safe with Jesus, praising Him for having loved you and saved you.[11]

How oft behind yon hill
The sun has hid his face!
How oft returned to fill
With joyful light the place!
And shall the sun for ever thus return?
Shall morn succeed to eve, and eve to morn?

O no, the day shall come,
(And who can tell how soon!)
When dark shall be that sun,
And red the silver moon;
When sun or moon shall never more return,
But God on clouds shall come the world to burn.

O, say, shall I be there,
To see the dreadful glare,
The dreadful sound to hear,
The dreadful heat to bear,
Of falling crags and rocks, of roaring seas,
Of smoking hills, and flaming earth and skies?

---

[9] 'The heavens shall pass away with a great noise, and the elements shall melt with fervent heat, the earth also and the works that are therein shall be burned up.' 2 Pet. 3:10.

[10] 'The heavens and the earth, which are now . . . are kept in store, reserved unto fire against the day of judgment and perdition of ungodly men.' 2 Pet. 3:7.

[11] 2 Thess. 1:6-10.

O yes, I shall be there;
The graves shall opened be;
All shall the trumpet hear,
The Judge's face shall see.
  In vain shall some upon the mountains call
  To hide their heads from Him who judges all.

The books shall then be read,
In which our God has wrote
All that we ever said,
Or ever did or thought.
  And many cheeks with burning shame shall glow,
  And many souls be plunged in deepest woe.

And how shall I escape
From endless misery?
My sins, a mighty heap,
Show I deserve to die.
  And yet to think upon that burning lake
  Makes my flesh tremble, and my bones to shake.

Lord, by the blood He shed
Who hung upon the tree,
Before the books are read,
May my sins pardoned be!
  And then my tears shall all be wiped away
  And I shall dwell in everlasting day.

Questions

- When will the last day come?
- What great noise will there be at the last day?
- What will Jesus say to all the dead people?
- What will be done to the bodies of people who love Jesus?

- Where will Jesus sit?
- What has Jesus written down in His books?
- Whose sins will Jesus forgive?
- Where has He written down their names?
- Where will God put the wicked?
- Who will torment them for ever?

The happiness of heaven

A verse from the Bible for you to learn

And God shall wipe away all tears from their eyes; and there shall be no more death, neither sorrow, nor crying, neither shall there be any more pain. Rev. 21:4.